Preface

Welcome to Value Forward's High Tech CEO Business Success System. Value Forward is one of the largest IT business-success advisement coaching firms in the world. The Value Forward Business Coaches is a coaching and executive management advisory group consisting of former CEOs and presidents of both public and private companies, senior company executives, and serial entrepreneurs.

As the CEO and founder of this group, I am linked to this team by a common business process called the Value Forward Success Method. The Value Forward Success Method is a proven process for you to grow your firm's top-line revenues, improve your marketing lead generation, maximize your operation department's success, increase organizational effectiveness, and reduce operating costs.

As senior-executive team advisement coaches, we focus on real world strategies that management teams can implement immediately to drive performance.

Success is defined in *Merriam-Webster's Dictionary* as "a: degree or measure of succeeding b: favorable or desired outcome; also: the attainment of wealth, favor, or eminence." This definition clearly characterizes what most CEOs of privately held and public companies seek. The combination of using measurement, attaining a defined outcome, and creating wealth is the foundation of the Value Forward's business growth system.

Why be successful without creating wealth? Why seek success without having a defined outcome or a measurable process? The Value Forward's approach to high tech success is based on researched action steps and best practice experiences.

Yes, strategy is important but without execution it is wasted thought. Great ideas are everywhere, but how many people act on those thoughts in a premeditated approach that maximizes their potential for profit and success? To be a successful high tech CEO, execution is more important than a great idea.

Marc Benioff, CEO and founder of salesforce.com did not invent the concept of capturing and managing customer data for marketing purposes, he just executed his business plan better. Bill Gates did not invent PC operating systems; he was just smarter than most on how to execute a market domination strategy. In contrast, Twitter CEO and founder Evan Williams has a great idea too, but so far, limited profits.

High Tech CEO Business Success Strategies

HIGH TECH

CEO

BUSINESS
—— SUCCESS ——
STRATEGIES

STRATEGY IS IMPORTANT,
EXECUTION IS BETTER!

By Paul DiModica

Publisher's Note

This book is designed to provide accurate and authoritative information in regard to the subject matter covered. It is sold with the understanding that neither the author nor the publisher is engaged in rendering legal, accounting, or other professional service. If legal advice or other expert assistance is required, the services of a competent professional should be sought.

First edition 2010
Second edition 2012
Third Edition 2013

ISBN 13 Digit: 978-1-933598-41-3

ISBN 10 Digit: 1-933598-41-7

Published by Johnson & Hunter, Inc.

Trademarks

Contents

By reading this book and completing the action steps at the end of each chapter, you will learn specific strategies for analyzing your business's current operational process, techniques to manage your department systems, and methodologies to increase marketing success and corporate profits. By implementing the action steps, you will have a process to examine where you are and where you want to be and a roadmap you can follow based on your personal and professional goals.

By taking your strategy and coupling it with our execution and management steps, you will minimize failure.

The Value Forward Group believes that in the high tech market you must *Hunt Now or Be Eaten Later*®. To hunt well, you must plot your course and execute a plan to find your profits.

This is an Action Step Book, Not a Good Read Book

There are lots of business books with theory and conceptual approaches that you read and ponder. This is not one of those books. This is a CEO business toolkit with specific tactics, strategies, and techniques to help you, the high tech CEO, become more successful—now.

How to Use This Book

You are going to be exposed to many methods, assessments, checklists, and action steps that will help you with your company success. I suggest that you read through the whole book once. Then go back to each chapter and absorb the material and implement the action steps listed throughout.

As stated in the subtitle, Strategy is Important, But Execution is Better. Thinking, analyzing, contemplating, researching, hypothesizing, and collectively discussing these recommendations with your executive management team, personal confidants, and investment advisors have relevance in your decision process.

But at the end . . . it's all about action.

Are all of these suggestions right for your company?

Only you will know. We have included multiple surveys in this book to help you decide what recommendations you need to deploy and which ones do not fit with your business or personal needs and objectives.

Some of our suggestions will seem obvious, some indigent; but we work with a very broad base of high tech companies with different ownership structures and principal goals, educations, annual revenues, business experiences, objectives, and management philosophies. So, use what you believe to be important and disregard that which is superfluous.

We wish you great business growth and hope you enjoy my book. Let me know how I can help.

Paul DiModica
CEO/Founder
Value Forward Group
www.ValueForward.com
pdimodica@valueforward.com
(770) 632-7647

Chapter 1

Introduction

Executive strategy without execution is wasted thought!

Implementing the Value Forward CEO Business Success Strategy System

For more than twenty-five years I have worked in high tech-based companies like yours. This journey has included Venture Capital funded companies, INC 500 players, privately funded start-ups, family run empires, new businesses launched by immigrants, and large public Fortune 1000 companies. During my career, I have worked as a Vice President of Operations/Engineering, a Senior Vice President of Sales and Marketing, Vice President of Strategic Development, Chief Operating Officer, and company founder in firms with annual revenues up to $900 million.

As I reflect on my career, I realize I have:

- Worked for an CEO who took his company to bankruptcy after he invented and dominated a U.S. market for ten years

- Worked with a company that had revenue growth of 100% for five straight years in a market where multiple competitors resided

- Worked for a high tech CEO who took money out of the company payroll account so he could vacation in Hawaii and then bounced payroll for his 180 employees

- Worked for a CEO and founder who was a marketing genius

- Worked with a CEO whose ego was larger than Mount Everest

- Interacted with venture capitalists who had never sold IT products or services and never had to make a business payroll; instead they had blue-blood résumés working at national consulting companies and/or graduated from an Ivy League MBA program

- Interacted with investment bankers tied to funding sources who became instant CEO coaches, always ready to give advice based on their experiences

- Worked for a public company whose division presidents ignored the CEO's directives because they were friends and former college roommates and knew that he would not hold them accountable to their assigned responsibilities

- Worked with marketing executives who thought PR and not sales was the way to increase corporate revenue in the business-to-business marketplace and convinced their technology CEOs to spend large amounts of investor funding on image campaigns that were worthless and created no revenue

This varied history, coupled with my current Value Forward Group experiences of consulting with hundreds of technology, software and professional firms (public and private) has allowed me to develop a best-practices approach on the strategic and tactical laws of growth that high tech CEOs need to use to stay in business and to increase their corporate revenues and profitability year over year.

The business survival rules that are in this book are based on personal experiences, proven best-practices analysis, third-party research, professional observation, and client occurrences. The recommended steps are not in any specific action order, because they all are important.

To be honest, many of these action steps will test your commitment to corporate growth. If you are a founder, your commitment to change your business to be successful and your assessment of your own skill sets as a manager and a leader will also be challenged as you ply your way through this publication.

The case studies are all true, but because of client confidentially, their business types, geographical locations, and IT offering descriptions all have been changed.

This book is designed for high tech CEOs who are seeking consistent year-over-year top-line revenue growth that is sustainable and overall business performance improvement.

This publication is not for the ego-sensitive business owner, the "It's my company and I can do anything I want with it" megalomaniac business principal, or the "I know everything that's why I am the CEO executive and the cash is mine—screw the employees" dictator. If you are one of these characters this is the wrong book. Get your money back, lock yourself in the cellar, and pretend you know what you are doing.

This book is for business owners, executive team members, company founders and CEOs who want to run a professional high tech organization that is profitable, scalable, and sellable at some time in the future. This book is for business executives who are open to outside best-practice suggestions and internal introspection on what their personal and professional needs and goals are.

To help you succeed at implementing the suggestions described in this book, each action step has a worksheet for you to use to start adjusting your current business model.

What Is High Tech Business Success?

Often management teams, both in public corporations and privately held high tech companies, measure business success through a numerical calculation of gross revenue and net-profit improvement. But this is a simplistic management approach when used singularly as a success measurement. At the Value Forward Group, we define the word *growth* from an external revenue-model approach as well as from an internal assessment of business methodology made by the management team's skill sets. Thus, true business growth and success only happen when internal management skills advance in parallel with top-line revenue enlargement. A more mature growth assessment of CEO success looks at the business-revenue capture model in its totality and at how all departments contribute holistically to overall business performance improvement.

In order to grow your business in a premeditated process you need to measure more than just year-over-year revenue increases. You must also consider the time management and operational productivity improvements made year over year, department by department, manager by manager to facilitate these gains. Revenue growth is often tied to the operational traffic capabilities inside your company.

Your firm's internal structure drives your strategy about the business offerings you create or resell, the identification of a prospect opportunity, the marketing communications you deploy, the sales procedures you implement, the sales process you use to close the sale, the sales delivery procedures you employ to fulfill orders, the accounts receivable collection you implement, the financial management model that funds your business, and the operational support variables needed to service clients.

Yet many businesses with poor internal operational management programs still grow their business revenue year over year. Why? Because increases in a company's revenue may be connected to unique anomaly drivers that are not replicable. So, when a management team's skill sets don't increase simultaneously with revenue or when the revenue jump stops, management is perplexed on what the next action step should be and success diminishes.

Examples of these anomaly revenue drivers include one salesperson out of a team of fifteen selling 90% of your sales, one customer representing 65% of your total revenue, or 80% of your total proceeds coming from contracted recurring-revenue streams like maintenance and support agreements that automatically renew. When these anomaly growth drivers are in place, they create an artificial sense of success and often incorrectly communicate to CEOs that they are doing their job well, when in fact their business and their business success is at risk.

Your personal strategy may be to sell your business next week, next year, or never, but the distinguishing characteristic between an entrepreneurially managed business process and a professionally managed business process are metrics and discipline and having all of your departments linked to a consistent method of revenue capture. This is not to say that the management team is not professional, but the process by which it is managed follows the path of an entrepreneur.

Danger: The Business Jungle Holds No Mercy For Any CEO Who Makes Mistakes

Managing a privately held family business or a corporate conglomerate is a challenging career choice frothed with financial risks, legal issues, extensive stress, difficult business decisions, and sometimes upset family members. Yet, as the Internet becomes a dominant distribution tool for many industries, more and more executives aspire for the top position in their current company or launch their own start-up based on hope, a dream, private funding, family requests, and/or their credit card.

As small and large companies navigate today's current economy, it is still surprising how many CEOs don't have a premeditated strategic plan with specific action steps they can execute. Look at the failures of Wall Street, automotive manufacturers, airline companies, banks, mortgage companies, and investment firms—all full of smart, well-educated business people who spent tens of millions of dollars annually getting advice from top-flight consulting firms on how to increase corporate success.

Yet they all failed. Why? Because the strategic recommendations given were not implemented by the management teams due to conflicting egos, corporate bureaucracy, being operationally unrealistic, or the advisement firm failed to supply specific executable action steps.

Most global 1000 companies use white-glove consulting firms to help their management teams develop a success strategy; however in many cases this approach fails. If you look at all of the recent corporate failures, you will find some large international consulting company lurking around. Why do these advisory firm engagements often fail? Usually for four reasons:

- CEOs of public companies hire global advisement firms as a protection filter when communicating new business strategy changes to their board of directors. By using a third-party consulting firm, CEOs can redirect the blame when business changes fail—it's not the recommendations that are important but instead the third-party written documentation.

- Many large companies use a Request For Proposal (RFP) to handle planned consulting contracts. This assumes the authors of the RFP (the management team) know what their business problems are and thus limits the upside success of any recommendation they might receive.

- Often white-glove consulting companies have long-term relationships with global 1000 clients. So, on a regular basis, advisement partners will ask their C-level executive contacts what areas they think they need help in, again making the assumption that the client has identified the problems.

- Many large consulting companies use the "Bus Model" of client management and support. They "bus in the A team" to sell and then "bus in the B team" to deliver—while the A team is selling to someone else.

This is not to say that white-glove consulting firms have no value because they do, but CEOs want action steps they can implement now.

If you have read any of my other books, attended our public seminars, received our newsletters, or worked with our team one-on-one, you will know that we are not fluffy, pie-in-the-sky, white-glove CEO advisors. Instead the Value Forward Group focuses on detailed action steps that are understood, can be used immediately, and are based on real-world success approaches.

We are a specialty CEO and management consulting company that focuses on using tactical and strategic methodologies that implement change. This publication is designed to be used as a guidebook to help CEOs implement successful action steps to minimize failure and increase potential for organic growth success.

Will the action steps recommended here be difficult for some high tech CEOs? Yes.

The Value Forward Group has worked with experienced and well-educated Global 100 management teams, Venture Capital funded CEOs, and family run presidents both in the private and public sector, but our primary focus is working with CEOs of privately held companies whose firms have annual revenues ranging between $1 million to $200 million. It is surprising how many senior staff executives will not implement all of the action steps in this book, and have thus missed great opportunities to enlarge their firm's revenues and profitability capacity.

Our focus is to help you increase your firm's success and organically grow your company by understanding action steps you can take to align operations, sales, marketing, financial management, and corporate strategy into one outbound revenue-growth model. At the Value Forward Group, we take a holistic approach to business building and, like a doctor, we do a health check on your entire business success model, not just one department.

There is an assumption by many executives (and their staffs as well) that just acquiring or buying a company, or being promoted into the title of CEO, implies that the CEO has deep strategic and tactical knowledge. Some do and some don't. But regardless of your experience level, this publication is designed to help you implement action steps *today* to help your firm *tomorrow*.

Chapter 2

History of the Value Forward Method

S o, where did the Value Forward success method come from and why will it work for you?

In 1984, after serving four years in the U.S. Navy, I left the service with an undergraduate degree in business administration and part of my MBA completed. I took an IT sales position in Boston, Massachusetts, for a Venture Capital (VC) funded high-tech company based in Toronto, Canada.

As I started my sales career, I was full of hope and anticipation of achieving great personal satisfaction from doing a job well and earning a large income. This Canadian company hired me to sell point-of-sales (POS) systems to restaurants and hotels. The position required me to sell POS systems that included software, hardware, cabling, training, and maintenance contracts as one integrated solution to independent restaurant owners in Boston.

The term *POS* was new to me and to most restaurant prospects in 1984. In fact, the more common term (although not technically a correct description for what we sold) was "cash registers."

Our POS system was state-of-the-art technology and had technical superiority over anything available in the market. It allowed restaurant employees to take customers' orders from the dining room and send them to printers in the kitchen with specific cooking instructions. Once the customers completed their meals, our system calculated tax, tips, and separate billings for each customer at a table and then allowed the waitstaff to "settle" the bill at the customer table through a unique process called "cashier banking." Cashier banking is where the waitstaff collects all of the money and credit card charges for the table assignments during their shift and then at the end of the day they close out their billings with the POS system (and the manager's approval).

These unique features eliminated the need for the cost of a cashier and expensive bar-coded printed checks, and increased the number of customers served on a shift (through more table turns) which increased the restaurant's total daily revenue.

Great Stuff! Unbelievable Technology—No Sales

Above and beyond the great features and functions of our software was our POS system's actual technical design. The system was a true Central Processing Unit (CPU) POS that operated off of an Intel 8086 chip, eight-inch floppy discs, and ran on Digital Research's CPM Operating System.

At the time, this was cutting-edge technology. Our system allowed us to operate up to twenty-five dumb POS terminals simultaneously without any speed or transaction problems. Pretty amazing for 1984!

But there were several problems. My high-tech management team forgot to mention a few things to me during my pre-employment sales interview, including:

- In 1984, most restaurant owners were afraid of computers and software.

- Restaurant owners hated too much technology because they liked the cash availability of their business and too much automation created an audit trail for the U.S. Internal Revenue Service (IRS) to follow.

- National Cash Register (NCR), a Fortune 500 company, had invented the cash register and had over 80% market share penetration in the restaurant industry.

- Our POS system cost 100% more than NCR's on an average proposal.

- Many independent restaurant owners worked 80 to 100 hours a week and were intimidated by slick sales approaches that seemed canned.

So, how was our firm going to grow its corporate revenue? How was I going to hit my annual sales quota ($1,000,000 in 1984 dollars), pay my mortgage, and keep my job?

During my first few weeks with this company, I received a week of company sales training, a week of product training, and did a ride-along with a sales manager for some prospect demos. I was told that if I was successful after the first year, I would be transferred to Hartford, Connecticut, and be promoted to a regional sales manager position. With this career goal dangled in front of me, I attacked my Boston territory, but within forty-five days of my hire date I was transferred to Hartford anyway (without a promotion).

As this Canadian IT company expanded across the U.S., I struggled with my selling and marketing strategy, the lack of company lead generation, and no documented corporate approach of why prospects should buy from us. Yet I had a $1 million sales quota to meet. During my first 90 days of employment, I struggled to figure out what I needed to do to hit my assigned target. After much thought and frustration, I came up with three basic questions that I, as a salesperson carrying a sales bag, needed to know.

- Why should prospects buy from me?

- Why would prospects not buy from me?

- How do I create value for my prospects that they will believe?

Simple questions—but when I asked my local management team and our corporate marketing vice president in Canada for some intellectual support on these questions, all I got were PR platitudes that never seemed to induce prospects to take an action step to buy. All I heard was "tell them we have the best system," or "we have the best support," or "they can save money on their costs of restaurant operations."

This was all management gobbledygook; non-productive corporate speak that made the communicators seem out of touch with what it took to sell in a competitive marketplace to buyers who were technically afraid of a system that was 100% more money than the Fortune 500 industry founder (NCR) that had 80% of the market share at that time.

At a meeting at corporate headquarters in Toronto, with all of the sales and marketing team members present, my CEO gave us a leadership pep talk about how superior our technology was and how we were going to be the next IBM of the restaurant industry. Great, but tell me how to sell this IT system now, how marketing is going to generate qualified leads for me, and better yet—tell me why my prospects should buy from us instead of NCR.

Also, tell me how to keep my job, hit my assigned sales quota (your manager gave me), and make some money!

A lot of expectations for a young buck salesperson.

After eleven weeks of no sales, no proposal negotiations, and handing out boxes of free company · marketing collateral, I decided to take some time off from my job (before I was fired) and think through the three questions that continued to trouble me.

After whining for a couple of days about poor me, I decided to take some action steps on my own.

I took off a week of pitching what I had to sell and talked with restaurant owners about their operational business problems, their personal needs as self-employed entrepreneurs, and why (or why not) they would spend money on technology. I wanted to know why they would spend $80,000 on a walk-in freezer or why they had someone build a custom Brazilian mahogany bar on premise for them for $150,000, and why they would not buy a technically superior POS system from me.

After I heard their responses, I sat down and developed my own sales and marketing methodology—out of fear of losing my job, to help me sell more, and to pay my mortgage. Using this self-developed sales and marketing approach, I went on to sell over $1.3 million (in 1984 dollars) of software, hardware, training, and maintenance contracts the first year and ended up getting promoted twice during my first twelve months of employment.

As my career advanced, I was promoted to Senior Vice President of Sales and Marketing, Vice President of Operations/Engineering, and Vice President of Strategy in various technology, software, and professional service companies with annual revenues up to $1 billion. As my experience evolved, I expanded the Value Forward High Tech Success Method to include analysis and assessments on corporate strategy, financial management, operations and development to increase revenue capture success.

During the late 1990s, I became the Vice President of Strategy Worldwide for a public company called Renaissance Worldwide. Renaissance had been originally called the Registry and was an IT staff aug and software project work company. Prior to my employment, the Registry had merged with a management consulting company called Renaissance Solutions which was widely known for the "The Balanced Scorecard," concept developed by David Norton, who was also President of Renaissance Solutions.

The foundational concept of the Balanced Scorecard is that management must align the four business process perspectives of Customers, Learning and Growth, Financial, and Internal Business Process to build growth.

It is estimated that over 70% of the Global 1000 public companies use a Balanced Scorecard strategy in some format in all or in parts of their operating business units. But, after being exposed to this scorecard concept and having the responsibility to evaluate our divisional success and the acquisitions we had made for the CEO of Renaissance Worldwide, I found a gap in the Balanced Scorecard theology of how to make a company successful.

From my experiences as a sales, marketing, strategy, and operations VP in different technology companies at different times, I knew that having great IT development and engineering departments meant nothing if you could not create revenue.

The Balanced Scorecard concept has tremendous merit, scholarship, and case studies behind it on why it works for well-established, large conglomerates—who are seeking to increase their business infrastructure management performance. But to use it as a tool to increase revenue growth is suspect, at best, for large companies and fails to address the needs of smaller companies, IT and otherwise, on how to build a replicable and scalable revenue-capture program.

In the high tech business market space:

PR is Not Revenue

Marketing is Not Revenue

Operations is Not Revenue

Advertising is Not Revenue

Branding is Not Revenue

Development is Not Revenue

Revenue is Revenue

So, taking my experiences based on my business success model development and assessing the analytical concepts and success gaps of the Balanced Scorecard, I created a new process we call the Value Forward Method or "the Revenue Capture Scorecard®."

Today, the Revenue Capture Scorecard is used in more than 100 countries by hardware and software application companies, SaaS and managed services players, telcos and VARs. What I learned from these early experiences is that revenue capture is the company's responsibility not just the sales team's responsibility—something one of my former CEOs did not know, never learned, and was ultimately fired for. High tech CEOs and business owners seeking to grow their top-line revenues and increase success must integrate all of their departments into one outbound revenue-capture program. Departments like engineering, operations, marketing, sales, financial management, and strategy must be aligned to maximize business growth.

You can't run a business like it's an extension of your own experiences. You need to know the specific reasons why prospects buy and don't buy and then integrate this information vertically into every department's approach and make it their operational DNA. Accept that you do not sell high tech products or services—rather you sell the *results produced by your technology offering* or the *business consequences or risks you protect prospects from.*

To grow your company organically and to build a replicable and scalable revenue-capture model, high tech CEOs must answer two stages of questions without ego, based on research, and in a format that your prototype buyer can understand and will respond to.

STAGE ONE QUESTIONS

1. Why would prospects buy from me?

2. Why would prospects not buy from me?

3. How do I create value for my prospects that they believe?

If you are a CEO of a privately or publicly funded firm, you have a fiduciary responsibility to know the answers to these questions and how this information should be used as revenue-capture tools for all of your departments to operate correctly. Don't just leave it up to the sales, marketing, and strategy departments to draw conclusions based on their assumptions. When answering these questions, you cannot give generic responses. You must be specific and granular. Don't guess. If you don't know, then you need to do customer research to determine exact answers.

Once you have the data, you need to integrate the answers into your marketing message, your sales process, your customer service and operational departments, and your overall corporate strategy and brand positioning.

STAGE TWO QUESTIONS

There are four reasons why prospects buy. **That's it. Only Four!**

1. How does your product or professional service increase the buyer's income (business-to-business market)?

2. How does your product or professional service decrease the buyer's expenses (business-to-business market)?

3. How does your offering manage the buyer's risks or consequences (business-to-business market)?

4. How does your offering make the buyer feel good (business-to-consumer market)?

By working through these four questions in stage two and combining your answers with the answers from the previous three questions in stage one, you now are ready to build a success program that is sustainable.

The answers to these seven questions hold the foundational knowledge you need to build your company into a sustainable, year-over-year growth business model.

CEO Success Action Steps

✓ To help you build scalable revenue-capture programs answer the following questions in detail with researched factual statements that are not emotionally attached to your ego. Do not answer based on a gut feeling.

1. Why do prospects buy from me?

2. Why do prospects not buy from me?

3. How do I create value that my prospects believe?

4. How does my offering increase income for the buyer (business-to-business market)?

5. How does my offering decrease expenses (business-to-business market)?

6. How does my offering manage business risks (business-to-business market)?

7. How does my offering make my buyers feel good (business-to-consumer market)?

✓ Once you answer these questions succinctly and without emotion and ego, you can build your corporate strategy, operations methodology, marketing communication, and sales processes to increase your targeted buyers' responses. **These questions and their answers are the framework for company success.**

Chapter 3

Assess Your Current Business Model

Oftentimes when working with senior executives, strategy and the "vision" thing seem to have independent lives of their own. Senior management teams love to strategize, develop grand mission statements, and create verbose customer service commitments that are publicly disseminated on their corporate website, listed inside their annual financial report, and even attached as a logo on the company shirt. This public communication of corporate strategy appeals to their right-brain thinking and allows them to separate themselves from the day-to-day minutia and tedious tasks required to manage a firm successfully.

If you want a great mission statement here it is:

> *Sell a competitive product or service where demand is greater than supply, and treat your employees, customers, and vendors fairly.*

Nothing else is needed. Stop wasting valuable management time with useless meetings focused on ego-reinforcing business philosophies that hang on a plaque in your office lobby.

**Yes strategy is important—
but strategy without execution is worthless.**

The world is full of great ideas, intensively documented business approaches, and detailed consultant reports on what you should do to increase your business success, but without action why waste your time?

Before we explore the successful action steps you should implement, please take the CEO Business Growth Success Test to help assess a benchmark of where your firm currently is as a business versus where it should be.

High Tech CEO Business Growth Success Test

1. Are your technology service, engineering, or operation departments set up as individual profit centers?

   ☐ Yes   ☐ No

2. Are your services, engineering, or operations departments' revenue-capture processes aligned and linked with the sales team's efforts?

   ☐ Yes   ☐ No

3. Do your development, engineering, or operations departments develop new products and services without market research, detailed project plans, or customer scopes?

☐ Yes   ☐ No

4. Has your operations/development department wrapped your services into a packaged offering with specific pricing to help your prospect buy easier?

☐ Yes   ☐ No

SALES QUESTIONS

5. Is the average success of your entire sales team assigned sales quota, or target, greater than 85%?

☐ Yes   ☐ No

6. Do you have a written step-by-step model detailing your firm's entire sales process from pre-sale to post-sale?

☐ Yes   ☐ No

7. Do you know your sales capture cost per sale?

☐ Yes   ☐ No

8. Do you track your lost sales analysis?

   ☐ Yes   ☐ No

9. Do you use a metric-driven method to mathematically calculate sales quotas or sales targets for your sales team?

   ☐ Yes   ☐ No

10. Do you pay your sales team the same commissions for new business from existing customers as you do for new business from new prospects?

    ☐ Yes   ☐ No

11. Do you know the lifetime dollar value of each of your top ten customers from the last five years?

    ☐ Yes   ☐ No

12. Do you and your management team get a detailed line item profit and loss statement (P&L) every month for each department, and every product and service you sell before corporate general and administrative costs (G & A)?

    ☐ Yes   ☐ No

13. Do you know specifically why your prospects buy from you (based on research, not conjecture)?

     ☐ Yes   ☐ No

14. Do you know specifically why you lose business (based on research, not conjecture)?

     ☐ Yes   ☐ No

15. Do you believe the senior management team members of your staff are qualified to help you double revenues during the next three years?

     ☐ Yes   ☐ No

MARKETING QUESTIONS

16. Do you increase your product or service pricing every year?

     ☐ Yes   ☐ No

17. Do you calculate marketing Return on Investment (ROI) for each of your marketing investments?

     ☐ Yes   ☐ No

18. Is your senior marketing manager paid financial incentives based on revenue growth?

☐ Yes   ☐ No

19. Does your marketing department have a written month-by-month marketing action plan listing each activity, its costs, and its expected inbound-lead generation goals?

☐ Yes   ☐ No

20. Has your firm calculated business demand for your technology products or services through market gap analysis?

☐ Yes   ☐ No

STRATEGY QUESTIONS

21. Are you growing your firm revenues organically or by acquisition?

☐ Organically   ☐ Acquisition

22. Is more than 50% of your current fiscal year revenue coming from existing customers?

☐ Yes   ☐ No

23. Do you believe that all of your customers buy from you based on price only?

☐ Yes   ☐ No

24. Do prospects call you and ask to buy your product or services without you contacting them first?

☐ Yes   ☐ No

25. Are your revenues up at least 15% from last year?

☐ Yes   ☐ No

ANSWERS

1. Yes	6. Yes	11. Yes	16. Yes	21. Organically
2. Yes	7. Yes	12. Yes	17. Yes	22. No
3. No	8. Yes	13. Yes	18. Yes	23. No
4. Yes	9. Yes	14. Yes	19. Yes	24. Yes
5. Yes	10. No	15. Yes	20. Yes	25. Yes

SCORING

Give yourself 4% for each correct answer. The test is not a complete assessment of your revenue-growth potential but a snapshot of where you may be versus where you need to be. How did you score?

60% and below
Your current high tech success business model cannot maintain year-over-year sustainable growth. If your

revenues are increasing, it is an anomaly, not a methodology or a business process, and has specific financial and operational leakage issues and corporate instability exposure.

To fix this position, you need to redesign your business and the integration of your operations, sales, marketing, and strategy processes into one revenue-capture approach.

61% to 80%

Your current business-growth model has some of the best-practice attributes needed to grow corporate revenue year-over-year using a planned process. Some of your business structure may need to be adjusted to maximize long-term corporate growth goals.

80% and above

Your business structure maximizes corporate growth capabilities and uses an inter-department alignment that focuses on strategy linked to action steps. You have built a sustainable pattern that should foster continued success for you and your team.

CEO SUCCESS ACTION STEPS

✓ Study the correct answers to this simple assessment. Decide what action steps you need to do to improve your firm's success score.

Chapter 4

Evaluate Your Management Style

I s your team or your management style stopping your growth? Do you have the right management team to take your company to the next level? Are your executives and team members learning on the job (and on your salary) or are they educated in growth strategies and tactics and moving you and your company forward?

> *Most business failures do not stem from bad times. They come from poor management, and bad times just precipitate the crisis.*
> *—Thomas P. Murphy*

Today many CEOs who operate as managers need to act as leaders. As a CEO, you need to understand the differences between managing and leading and know which areas you need to improve on. Review this list of comparisons to see where you fit and to decide whether you are a leader or a manager.

1. **Direction**
   Managers supervise, control, and correct.

   Leaders strategize, inspire, and motivate.

2. **Goals**
   Managers focus on short-term goals, plodding through an endless series of internal processes.

   Leaders think and act like owners, recognizing the importance of long-term goals, vision, and value-added functions.

3. **Thinking Style**
   Managers are satisfied with incremental gains, being just a little better than the competition. They judge success solely by the bottom line.

   Leaders redefine their markets and constantly search for knowledge from new places, new markets, and new customers.

4. **Communication**
   Managers engage in a lot of one-way communication, giving orders or having people report to them.

   Leaders encourage free-flowing interactive communication and are receptive to feedback, both positive and negative.

5. **Perspective**
   Managers prefer specific, functional expertise.

   Leaders see the interdependencies between functions and processes and endorse a general management perspective.

6. **Education Style**
   Managers define themselves by perpetual activity, generating transactions, attending meetings, walking factory floors, etc.

   Leaders get things done, but also take time to reflect and develop their sixth sense, because they know a well-seasoned sixth sense can be more valuable than mounds of data when it comes to making good decisions.

7. **Emotion**
   Managers are analytical and coolly detached.

   Leaders produce emotional energy, the kind that inspires and motivates people.

8. **Faith**
   Managers are firm believers in Murphy's Law, so they constantly monitor their employees.

   Leaders maintain a high level of trust and commitment with their people.

9. **Openness**

   Managers need everything proven and take great pride in their ability to say no to ideas that don't meet their standards.

   Leaders embrace diversity and are highly receptive to ideas and people who are different. They realize that new, young, original, or off-the-wall ideas could evolve to become the cutting-edge solution that is needed.

10. **Feedback**

    Managers place conscious and unconscious limits on what they are willing to say or listen to.

    Leaders recognize that clear and honest communication is essential in today's fast-paced business world and are open to both positive and negative feedback.

9 Ways CEOs Manage (or Lead) Their Business and Employees

After working with hundreds of companies and thousands of employees, the Value Forward Group has identified eight common types of CEO management styles. These styles are not always reflective of the company's size but more on how individual CEOs manage their firms.

Each of these management models has positive and negative attributes for employees and management teams. To help you discover where you are in the business model and to determine how your leadership style affects your team members, review these descriptions:

1. **CEO Maintenance Management Model, Family-Run**

    Top-line revenues are flat or have been decreasing for three years or more. This leadership model is a family-run business that is ten-plus years old where usually more than one person (husband/wife; father/daughter; mother/son, etc.) is or has been on the payroll. Instead of investing in their business assets (sales, marketing, operations, inventory, technology), management is milking cash flow to use the company's revenue stream as a retirement program. Often these executives take long vacations, don't come into the office very often, and generally cruise along. This management style, rightly earned by the principals who took the business risks to launch the company, has a negative impact for employees seeking to maximize their income and career opportunities in a growth-directed firm.

2. **CEO Growth-Mode Management Model, Family-Run**

    This management team (although dominated by family members) understands that it must invest in the business, either to propitiate future generations of family cash-flow contributions or simply a desire to become more successful. It is often a positive work environment for employees and compensation plans are competitive or more generous than Global 1000 companies. This leadership style can provide a great place to work, but may limit senior management promotions due to family members' ownership and extended employment opportunities for upcoming generations.

3. **CEO Investor/Wall Street Management Model**
   This management team drives its company based on the commitment it has made to VCs, private investors, or Wall Street. They invest in their employees based on how close the company has hit its financial obligations or milestones. If they miss their numbers, they adjust the staff head count regardless of business need. This model is driven by executives who seek financial confirmation not an understanding of how those numbers are achieved. This leadership style is emotionally reactive and driven by management's sense of its own employment security rather than planned business logic.

4. **CEO Global 1000 Farmer Management Model**
   Most Global 1000 firms use a farmer management style of leadership: instead of taking calculated risks, corporate bureaucracy overwhelms them and they simply focus on selling more technology and professional services into their existing customer base. It is a short-term solution, easy to implement,

and cautious in its approach; yet it creates an artificial perception of success controlled by the current customers' ability to buy. For employee team members, it is usually an easy operating model to function under. Usually compensation is not competitive with more aggressive players and is limited in the long-term as customers buy less. Companies in this mode focus more on brand selling than new inbound-lead generation.

5. **CEO Global 1000 Hunter Management Model**
   This is the management model of choice, not common, but definitely on the rise internationally and to some degree domestically in the U.S. CEOs with this management style continue to make investments in new business process, new technology and professional services, and company acquisitions that open up new markets and additional offerings. This is a great work environment for employees because compensation plans are usually very aggressive and these companies supply team members with all of the marketing and support services they need to be successful.

6. **CEO Product or Service Superiority Management Model**
   The product superiority management model is dominated by a CEO or founder who has a background or education in technical and/or engineering areas and actually believes that superior technical capabilities in today's market is why

prospects buy. This is a difficult management model to operate under because the senior management team does not understand sales or marketing methodology and expects employees to tell customers how great their product is. Often this leadership focuses on building better technical offerings without studying market demand or market gaps and assumes that if they build it, prospects will buy. Compensation for team members is usually average or slightly below average as executives spend a disproportionate amount of revenue on R&D.

7. **CEO Entrepreneur Growth Management Model**
   Like its sister management model, the Global 1000 Hunter Model, the entrepreneur growth management model is an aggressive leadership process that actively seeks to grow a company based on continuous process improvement and alignment of sales, marketing, strategy, and R&D. It is often led by a founder who is seeking fast growth but not interested in an IPO in the short-term. This is a great company to work for because it usually pays its salespeople very well, supports all departments with a strong *esprit de corps* attitude, and provides upward mobility based on achievement.

8. **CEO Partner Model**
   This leadership model often has the same management characteristics as the CEO Maintenance Management, Family-Run model

because of the interrelationship of the partner owners. When high tech businesses start, most partners have the same common objectives and exit strategies. But as the firm matures and each partner's responsibilities evolve into more specific department executive authority, chasms often develop based on work ethic, compensation equity, and company exit strategies frustrating each partner in different ways. This frustration then trickles down amongst the employees who observe and assimilate the partners' lack of corporate executive continuity and reduces their productivity and perception of long-term career growth. This leadership model usually reduces the long-term success of the firm, unless the partners manage their frustration visibility to their staff.

9. **CEO Hybrid Management Model**
   This model is usually a combination of Entrepreneur Growth Management and a Growth Mode Management Model Family-Run or an Investor/Wall Street Management Model. Either way, it is a positive environment for team members seeking to work in a dynamic environment and receive compensation based on their value not some arbitrary calculation.

In 1969, Dr. Laurence Peters wrote a seminal book titled *The Peter Principal.* In it, he describes how management teams often promote employees into new positions above their level of competency which ultimately causes them to fail.

- Has your firm ever promoted a great salesperson into sales management so it would not lose the revenue that salesperson generated?

- Has your senior management team ever hired or promoted a marketing person into an executive position because he was personable, well-liked by his peers, and created great-looking brochures?

- Has your firm ever recruited an executive manager away from a competitor (whom you continually lost business to) just because that person became available and your firm believed it needed "a player" on its team?

Just because a salesperson hits his or her assigned sales quota does not mean he or she is going to be a good sales manager or vice president of sales. Just because your brochures are appealing does not mean your marketing manager understands how to do market gap analysis and market research correctly to help direct your company's future. So when promoting company employees, it is important to manage them as assets that contribute to your growth factor.

When growing your high tech company, in both recessionary and non-recessionary times, there are specific action steps you need to take to grow your revenue once you have identified a business opportunity. These action steps must manage both internal and external growth factors that either accelerate or depress your company's growth.

INTERNAL BUSINESS GROWTH FACTORS THAT MUST BE MANAGED

- Management team

- Existing customers

- Employees

- Suppliers and partners

EXTERNAL BUSINESS GROWTH FACTORS THAT MUST BE MANAGED

- The economy

- New customers

- Government regulations

- Competitors

Usually management looks internally to its team to help take the company to the next level. But this leadership model—which uses *only* the company's internal knowledge set—sometimes actually reduces growth potential because the team has *never been* where you want to go. If your team could get you to the next level, you would already be there.

To grow corporate revenue, the four primary Internal Growth Factors of management, old customers, employees, and suppliers must all be aligned succinctly with *premeditated* growth steps and managed simultaneously with the external growth factors of the economy, new customers, government regulations, and competitors. And, you must have the right team members working with you. If your management team has been promoted prematurely or does not have in-depth knowledge of industry best-practices and business growth methods your expansion potential is limited.

So, when defining and building out your business growth, make sure your team members' capabilities contribute to your objectives. Don't promote based on need, instead hire based on a candidate's previous experiences and his or her ability to take you to the next level.

In today's economy, your employees are one of the most expensive and least predictable business assets you have.

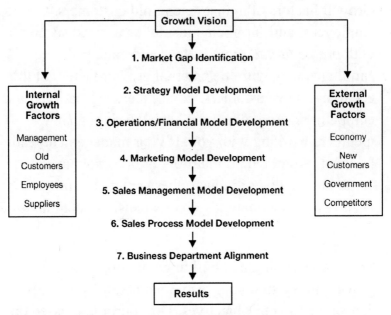

Value Forward Business Growth System

Growth Vision

1. Market Gap Identification
2. Strategy Model Development
3. Operations/Financial Model Development
4. Marketing Model Development
5. Sales Management Model Development
6. Sales Process Model Development
7. Business Department Alignment

Results

Internal Growth Factors

Management

Old Customers

Employees

Suppliers

External Growth Factors

Economy

New Customers

Government

Competitors

Business growth is a company responsibility.

> *The best corporate leaders never point out the window to blame external conditions; they look in the mirror and say 'We are responsible for our results!'*
> *—Jim Collins, Author of Good to Great*

Once you have selected the right management team members to help your firm grow and avoided Peter Principle candidates, you then want to protect this asset by increasing their personal productivity and job satisfaction. Here are seven tips to accomplish this.

7 Motivational Tactics to Increase Employee Productivity (and Maximize Your Investment) Without Giving a Raise

- Send handwritten notes to employees every month thanking them for their help. These notes should be short, to-the-point, non-flowery, and sincere.

- Send restaurant gift certificates to employees who do a good job.

- Create unique management job titles for employees to make them feel good.

- Send thank-you gifts to spouses (flowers to women, movie tickets to men) to thank them for the spouses' contributions to the company.

- Institute an Employee of the Month award. Announce winners at a company meeting or through the corporate newsletter.

- Give employees an office with a door.

- Establish an over-the-top employee of the month trophy, like a martial arts trophy, and have it passed along month to month

CEO SUCCESS ACTION STEPS

✓ Decide what type of CEO you are:
  ☐ Manager ☐ Leader

✓ Decide what type of business model you operate in.

✓ Review by the internal and external factors needed to grow your business and build a process to manage them by.

✓ Avoid Peter Principle employee promotions.

Chapter 5

Examine Your Method of Growth and the Affect It Has on Your Business Success

S ustainable year-over-year growth in the product and service space is a continuous challenge for management teams seeking to expand their business. Business expansion is tied to the market model you select for both your current success and future expansion and its correct alignment with one of the four growth cycles your firm currently resides in (start-up stage, growth stage, mature stage, and decline stage).

At the Value Forward Group, we have identified **six primary models** for business growth that can be deployed to increase corporate revenue. Each of these models has both positive and negative attributes that must be managed. Additionally, each one of the primary approaches can be applied to more than one product or service within the same company using a best-practices approach to benchmark your success.

The selection and implementation of the method you choose is a strategic decision that requires an analytical approach to balance both current cash-flow needs and future corporate goals.

The key to growing your firm is to align the business-growth method you select with your firm's current business life cycle. Often companies do not correctly match their growth method with the right business life cycle and then wonder why they are not maintaining year-over-year sustainable growth.

As a CEO, you must decide which growth model (or combination of models) you are going to use to increase your business success. A haphazard unpremeditated growth model is a sloppy business model that impedes success.

6 COMMON BUSINESS GROWTH MODELS

1. **Market Duplication**. This growth model focuses on paralleling your product or service pricing, features, and business offerings based on your direct competitor's business model.

   Examples: Oracle and SAP, HP and IBM

   Strengths of this growth model:

   - Buyer education is minimal

   - Shorter sales cycles due to increased buyer knowledge

- Reduced marketing costs as compared to unique offering launches

- Less market gap analysis research required

Weaknesses of this growth model:

- Difficult to communicate offering uniqueness

- Price points will feel pressure and can be commodity driven

2. **The Market Variation Model.** This model is based on the competition's business approach but adjusts to it visibly by offering prospects some improvement in product or service value, feature, price, or distribution model.

   Examples: Saleforce.com and Siebel, Sony and Apple

   Strengths of this growth model:

   - Larger gross margin available

   - Educated buyer

   - Shorter Sales Cycles

   Weaknesses of this growth model:

   - Must steal market share from existing industry leaders

- Competitors change often, forcing you to always play catch up with value differences

3. **Market Symbiotic Attachment**. This model is used by firms whose revenue streams are connected directly to the success or failure of other technology vendors. It is often used by VARS and resellers.

   Examples: Microsoft Gold Partners and IBM Partners

   Strengths of this growth model:

   - Company succeeds based on the strength of the attachment company's success

   - Often co-op advertising funding is available

   - Company can reduce marketing expenditures due to the attachment company's visibility and branding identification

   Weaknesses of this growth model:

   - Company success can be diminished if the partner company's offering is perceived to be of less or minimal value

   - Business margins can be reduced due to oversupply of the same channel partners in your market, vertical industry, or selling geography

- Value of partnership is diminished if prospects perceive that your alignment is a volume position versus a unique position

- Company's business valuation is usually low because the firm's intellectual property belongs to its partner company

4. **Market Consolidation.** This model uses a growth process where vendors buy up or roll up revenue by buying other companies and their market share without using internal organic growth techniques (e.g., Computer Associates).

Examples: CSA, Oracle

Strengths of this growth model:

- Can increase market share quickly

- Can grow top line revenue at an accelerated rate

- Can buy distribution channels to roll out new offerings

- Can increase gross margins and support maintenance fees due to fewer competitors in the market and market domination potential

Weaknesses of this growth model:

- Can alienate current customer base and acquired customer base due to increased pricing changes

- Organizational infrastructure may be too stressed to handle new acquisitions profitably

- Acquisition growth may hide the company's organic sales and marketing weaknesses

5. **Market Innovation.** This growth strategy takes market variation a step further. Instead of a singular market variation, this model creates a new market paradigm by creating a new offering that changes the current industry approach.

Example: Apple iPhone4 and Amazon

Strengths of this growth model:

- Higher gross margins and sales price opportunities

- Market first-mover position allows for market domination opportunities

Weaknesses of this growth model:

- Easy for me-too competitors to enter market

- Company must continue to invest in innovation to maintain market share

6. **Market Entrepreneurial Launch.** This model of growth happens when firms use market gap analysis and identify new opportunities where market demand is greater than supply.

Examples: Goto and Overture (invented Pay-Per-Click Advertising)

Strengths of this growth model:

- Large margins for high tech offering on launch

- Reduced PR costs due to viral marketing opportunities

- Accelerated revenue capture due to first-mover position

Weaknesses of this growth model:

- High development costs

- High marketing costs

- Time market can be elongated

Some companies use several growth models, depending on how their management teams attack the market; but generally, based on our research, there is usually one dominant business growth methodology used that has secondary influences on how the firm deploys its growth model for each stage of growth

As your offering or company in totality moves into a new business cycle stage, you must reposition your sales team demographic profile (as well as your marketing and strategy position).

Each one of these six growth options can be used to increase your firm's revenue as a whole or you can develop a targeted unique market model for *each* product and service you sell, based on your company's business success strengths and objectives. Sometimes a firm may have multiple business growth models running in parallel for multiple offerings, juggling the unique characteristics needed for each to succeed.

Understanding the strengths of your current core competence and business assets (i.e., human capital, intellectual capital, strategic partnerships, sales and marketing skill sets, operational develop capabilities, brand perception by targeted prospects, etc.) affects your ability to manage your selected growth strategy correctly.

The key to selecting the right high tech growth model for your firm is **finding the intersection** between your company's product or service life cycle and your business growth cycle. When these two business cycles intersect correctly, companies grow. When these two cycles run in opposing directions, company marketing costs are high, sales capture capabilities becomes stagnant or decrease, and development costs erode margins.

What business growth model are you using to grow your company?

Are you deploying a business success model that matches your corporate objectives? Did you select your current success model through an authoritative research process? Was it a well-planned thought process?

Or are you operating inside a business model that you fell into or evolved into that is restricting your potential upside growth?

Does your current model match your current offerings life cycle and your company's business growth cycle?

If not, then maybe one reason your firm is not growing at the Performa level you had anticipated is that you are trying to sell red shoes to blue shoe buyers.

CEOs need more courage to change their business models.

Oftentimes when advising CEOs, we end up discovering that their firm's inability to grow year over year in any economic market is tied to their incorrect selection of the business growth model—not the product or service they market or the price point they sell at.

CEOs need to change their business models based on their primary corporate objectives . . . even when it is difficult!

Senior management teams need to actively investigate and pursue new business models that produce growth results—not average results, but dramatic over-the-top revenue-changing results that shift their business paradigm. Accepting 5%, 10%, or even 15% annual growth in today's market space and economy is really just giving up to the status quo—**just hanging on.**

Fear of the unknown, generated by change or acceptance of the current operating model, causes the executive team to accept its destiny of slow growth or "manageable" growth.

But, to build a sustainable business success advantage, you must continually focus on the business model implemented.

A CEO in the IT business is like a Navy Seal—he must adapt to his environment, change, or die.

So, forget everything you've read in your favorite business magazine about how "other" successful IT companies are managing their business model. **They are not you.** Their financials, market competition, intellectual property, development techniques, sales distribution, and marketing models are diametrically different than yours. They are not you . . . and you are not them.

To really succeed, with a structured best-practices approach to growth, focus on how you can grow your firm based on your business strengths and weaknesses and your company's known core competencies and selecting the right business growth model that meets your company's objectives.

> *The most fatal illusion is the settled point of view. Life is growth and motion; a fixed point of view kills anybody who has one.*
> *—Brooks Atkinson*

It takes a committed effort to accept that your current business model may not be enough.

It takes "business courage" to change.

Courage is a funny word. It creates "visual brochures" in the mind of the receiver based on his or her perception of what it means. "Courage," as Aesop once said, "is easy from a safe distance."

CEOs must look beyond what Wall Street tells them or what their investors want . . . the "Steady Eddy," grow-as-you-go concepts must be ignored. You can always blame the economy or your competitors for dropping their prices, or the sales team; but innovative CEOs who are growth-directed take chances and adapt to their business model needs. Yes, it is safe and easy not to take chances and grow slowly, but CEOs need to stop managing their companies from a safe distance.

This type of cultural and operational change requires CEO courage.

Sometimes I wonder—where are the hard-charging, take-no-prisoners CEOs who want to dominate their market?

Is Larry Ellison of Oracle the last CEO success samurai?

You don't have to like Ellison, but you can recognize the fire (and feel it if you're his competitor) in his business approach to growth and success.

It seems as though the dot-com explosion, Wall Street pressure, and the Sarbanes-Oxley Act sapped all of the strength out of the let's-go-get-the-business CEOs. This lack of go-get-'em leadership trickles down to the sales, operations, finance management, and marketing teams. They observe the senior management team's lack of aggressive leadership and subliminally adopt the passive style of revenue acquisition and client management.

It is estimated there are 150,000 high tech firms in North America with five or more employees and at least 1,000,000 firms worldwide with five or more employees. As a senior executive, if you are not aggressively growing your business, thousands of other companies are calling your prospects, stealing your market share, developing new code at a lower cost per hour, and screaming over the Internet that they are the new dog on the street who *your prospects should buy from.*

Worse, in today's economy, your competition is not only other high tech firms, but other non-competitor business investments your prospects are considering.

Technology has to prove to prospects that it is a business tool that produces results. You have to compete for budget allocation with other non-IT purchases. Restaurant prospects are trying to decide on your new point of sale system or a new walk-in freezer. Manufacturing companies are trying to make a decision between your new assembly line software automation applications or five new trucks.

This dual competitor environment of competing with other companies and non-IT purchases screams that business growth models in the high tech industry have to be living, breathing processes that are adaptable and adjusted as needed to deal with the economic market and the near-term changes that will continue to be required to stay successful.

Is it naïve for me to suggest that CEOs take control of their companies, not maintain the same old operating models, and try to aggressively grow their firms even if it is culturally, financially, or politically uncomfortable?

Yes, if the CEO's goal is to maintain current status quo.

No, if the CEO's goals are to lead his or her firm to great success year after year.

Is Your Company Supply-Driven or Market-Driven?

Do you sell technology or professional services based on your perception that there is a huge market? Is your market potential based on the observations of your competitors? Often, high tech companies reactively expand their capabilities based on assumptions, research and development payback requirements, local sales success, and the personal experiences of a founder who "knows" the market.

But, is this a scalable, replicable, and sustainable business model?

Buyer demand normally falls into two operational patterns. Which one does your company operate from?

A Supply-Driven Business Model is when a company creates, markets, and supplies what it sells **without** a thorough knowledge of buyer needs or market gap demand.

A Demand-Driven Business Model responds to prospects' needs, requirements, and business expectations based on their wants and desires.

For CEOs to increase corporate growth, they must become a demand-driven not supply-driven organization. To determine what type of firm you are, take a quick audit to see if your firm is demand-driven or supply-driven.

1. Does your firm forecast sales based on market gap analysis?
   ☐ Yes   ☐ No

2. Have you separated your current business markets or industries into sub-segments based on segment profitability?
   ☐ Yes   ☐ No

3. Are your current business segments each growing at least 5% in total aggregate demand per year in the regions you currently sell into?
   ☐ Yes   ☐ No

4. Are your operating margins within your business segments lower this year than last year?
   ☐ Yes   ☐ No

5. Do you use a market percent capture calculation model (e.g., 3% of $100,000,000 national market) to forecast your sales potential?
   ☐ Yes   ☐ No

6. Did you create your new product or service before you investigated the market demand for its sales distribution?
   ☐ Yes   ☐ No

7. Do prospects buy your product or service because your pricing is lower than your competitor(s)?
   ☐ Yes   ☐ No

8. Is your marketing plan older than six months?
   ☐ Yes   ☐ No

9. Does your firm use the same sales model and selling vernacular to market each business segment?
   ☐ Yes   ☐ No

10. Do prospects call you and ask to buy your product or service?
    ☐ Yes   ☐ No

ANSWERS

1.	Yes	6.	No
2.	Yes	7.	No
3.	Yes	8.	No
4.	No	9.	No
5.	No	10.	Yes

SCORING

Give yourself 10% for each correct answer. The higher your score, the more demand-driven your firm is. The more demand-driven your company is, the higher the potential for sustainable success you will have.

CEO SUCCESS ACTION STEPS

✓ Select one of the six business success growth models discussed that your firm is currently using and identify the growth model(s) you wish to move your firm to.

✓ Determine the time frame needed to accomplish this transition.

✓ Assess if you are demand-driven or supply-driven.

Chapter 6

Use Market Gap Analysis to Expand Your Offerings

It's marketing gap—not product or service superiority!

You love what you sell, but how do you know there is a market demand for it? Is it because some buyers have bought it? Is it because your competitors sell it (maybe they are not very smart)?

Do you know how many buyers there are locally, regionally, and nationally?

Do you believe that because your product or service is so superior, buyers will flock to buy it? Or do you just have a gut feeling?

These perceptions dominate management team and CEO discussions in small and large companies when they are seeking to acquire a new product or service, or launch technology offerings their company has developed.

As companies move forward, they are consistently challenged with making investment decisions on which new geographic markets to expand into, what new business verticals to compete in, and what type of product or service they need to develop and sell. Incorrect decisions can waste investment funding and delay time to market, or worse, create corporate chaos that affects the very foundation of the firm's financial stability.

One way to minimize incorrect business decisions is through the use of Market Gap Analysis as a decision tool to help executive teams identify and validate the potential for new market opportunities, current market penetration success capabilities, and investment criteria for new product or service options.

What Is Market Gap Analysis?

Market Gap Analysis focuses on using a systematic research approach to discover and uncover sales opportunities **where market demand is greater than supply**. Used extensively in the business-to-consumer market space (B2C), it can help your firm identify, quantify, and select business market segments that are currently under-serviced.

Through the deployment of Market Gap Analysis, your firm can make logical strategic and tactical decisions based on market facts, not subjective opinion. Market Gap Analysis is a proactive approach to identify market demand.

How Is Market Gap Analysis Different From Market Research?

Market Research focuses on the investigation and analysis of known business model characteristics including sales, marketing, distribution, and deployment techniques whereas Market Gap Analysis investigates unknown business model opportunities through a step by step process. Market Research does not identify new markets where demand is greater than supply whereas Market Gap Analysis does. Market Research is a reactive approach to help understand how you position, sell, and distribute technology and professional services into an existing market where demand is already determined (or perceived to be determined)—Market Gap Analysis is a proactive approach to identify new markets.

Why Should A Firm Use Market Gap Analysis?

The key to successful top-line revenue growth is to identify a demand that is unfulfilled and then create (or acquire) products or services that you can sell to fill this gap. Many firms have NEVER done market gap analysis and, in fact, they are currently failing to sell *their* programs and services successfully due to this oversight.

Traditionally, firms use the following three methods to forecast demand:

- The percentage rule of market research method instead of market gap analysis to determine sales opportunities. (Take the national market statistics of an industry and assume that you will sell a percentage of the total market, i.e., 2% of CRM). Overconfident perceptions of market demand are generated through this method and can lead to flattened sales, decreased gross operating margins, and incorrect sales forecasts.

- Assume there is a market gap based on the firm's experience.

- Believe the product or service they sell (and have invested in) is so great, it will have buyers. This method is oftentimes associated with author's pride or developer's pride.

In all of these examples, a firm may actually achieve some increase (a false market gap analysis) in corporate revenues in a launch mode that ultimately misguides management even further to increase their investment based on their early success. Ultimately, as they try to expand their business in this way, they fail and do not understand why.

When Should A Firm Use Market Gap Analysis?

A Market Gap Analysis should be used when the firm is:

- Looking to forecast and confirm demand for an existing product or service
- Seeking to enter a new business vertical or industry
- Trying to decide on the investment needed to expand a department
- Seeking to merge or acquire another firm
- Deciding to launch a new product or service

It is not what you sell that determines your success—it is what prospects will buy!

CEO SUCCESS ACTION STEPS

✓ Calculate market gap opportunities for each product and service you sell (example below).

Product One:_____

Market Gap	☐ Yes	☐ No
Local	☐ Yes	☐ No
Regional	☐ Yes	☐ No
National	☐ Yes	☐ No

Product Two:_____

Market Gap	☐ Yes	☐ No
Local	☐ Yes	☐ No
Regional	☐ Yes	☐ No
National	☐ Yes	☐ No

Service One:_____

Market Gap	☐ Yes	☐ No
Local	☐ Yes	☐ No
Regional	☐ Yes	☐ No
National	☐ Yes	☐ No

Service Two:_____

Market Gap	☐ Yes	☐ No
Local	☐ Yes	☐ No
Regional	☐ Yes	☐ No
National	☐ Yes	☐ No

Chapter 7

Market Vertically for Strategic Organic Growth

Whenhigh tech CEOs look at a map of the United States or the world and think "that is our market," it is a non-studied approach to market identification. When companies start out, cash is king and business principals often take any and all deals to stimulate funding. Horizontal marketing to unlimited vertical industries is the model practiced by many who believe that segmenting business markets limits revenue-capture opportunities.

But, this perception is contradictory to best-practice studies for business growth.

In fact, vertical industry marketing is the only viable option technology and professional service businesses have today to sell more while reducing their marketing costs and increasing their gross margin. Why? Because focusing on your business model results in increased revenue.

The big secret in marketing: to become horizontal, you must dominate vertically first.

Vertical industry marketing benefits include:

- Reduced operations, engineering, and service delivery costs

- Reduced marketing costs

- Reduced salesperson frustration

- Increased knowledge of the product, service, and industry by the sales team

- Improved sales closing ratios

- Shortened sales cycle

- Reduced prospect training time

- Increased gross margin

- Increased corporate profitability

By tightening your market focus, you control both fixed and variable costs by itemizing your expenses for each individual business vertical you operate in.

How to Verticalize Your Company

After performing a Market Gap Analysis, select three business verticals or industries the analysis findings have identified as unserviced then determine which of your offerings fit these gaps. After you own and dominate these three markets, add a new business vertical as needed one at a time. Once you control five or six business vertical industries, you now have become horizontal.

Often CEOs are concerned that transitioning to a vertical market sales model will, in the short-term, reduce their corporate revenues. To manage this transitional model timeline, focus on three outbound business verticals for all of your sales and marketing investments. When the leads are inbound from verticals that you do not proactively sell to, take any qualified ones you get and sell them, but put all of your effort and investments into outbound marketing on your selected business verticals. As a high tech CEO, tighten your focus by selling more to less markets (that are large enough to support you) and your increased success will be at your door.

CEO SUCCESS ACTION STEPS

✓ Make a list of three outbound markets/industries to sell.

✓ Focus <u>only</u> on these three outbound markets.

✓ Only expand into a new business vertical where market gap demand is greater than supply and only enter one market at a time.

Chapter 8

Track Your Marketing Return on Investment

It's not marketing expenditure—it's lead generation and sales!

To help me understand a company's operational marketing environment, I ask all of my clients the following three questions:

- What are your marketing costs per lead?

- What is your return on investments for your tradeshow expenditures?

- What is your customer conversion ratio (CCR) of your unique visitors to prospect/buyer conversions from your website home page?

Nine times out of ten, I get a blank stare—like a deer in headlights. If I get an answer at all, it is a guess, not a factual statement—usually, some fabricated answer by a marketing manager who is trying to look informed in front of their CEO. Yet every CEO of a start-up, established player, and mature business enterprise spends money on marketing because they see marketing as a tool to generate revenue. They believe they need beautiful, four-color brochures, slick websites, and smart branding to professionally represent their firms' value. Spending money on marketing is a business necessity. Yet year in and year out management teams spend large sums of money on marketing programs that have no traceable return on investment. Marketing has one primary function: to create inbound leads and buyers. That's it.

Understanding the Importance of Calculating Marketing ROI

In the Value Forward Marketing program, all departments are expected to be direct contributors to the profitability of the firm. Historically, the marketing department has been a staff position in support of the line position of sales. Through this traditional relationship (depending on the size of the firm), the VP of Marketing or the senior marketing person reports to the Senior VP of Sales and Marketing or maybe a Chief Operating Officer (COO).

Most marketing managers have evolved from a traditional marketing and communications background that includes graphic design, press management, copywriting, tradeshow supervision, and sometimes direct mail. In the digital economy, some managers even have B2B interactive experience (more common in B2C) with e-mail, eZine and Webinars.

As the Internet evolves, it has become a critical selling medium that can produce sales transactions and qualified leads. Thus, expectations and compensation for marketing executives must be expanded to encompass the Web. With their increased responsibility, marketing managers need to be held accountable to a budgeted monthly revenue quota, *just like the sales department, with the same expected ROI.*

The purpose of this integrated marketing program is to tie all senior managers directly to corporate revenue goals that are *mutually managed by all department heads as a group quota.* By elevating the status, responsibilities and compensation of marketing management, you reinforce their partnership in revenue capture with the sales department and the company as a whole.

Is this a new direction for most firms? **Yes.**

Is this the future for companies that seek to have an integrated outbound-revenue capture machine? **Yes.**

How do you accomplish this? First, you must determine how the marketing department will be held accountable to quantifiable revenue contribution and ROI.

In setting up your marketing department as a sales contributor to the corporate-revenue forecast, it is necessary for you to calculate its costs to your firm using a traditional ROI model.

Let's look at the cost of sales and the potential ROI, and then use it as a benchmark against the investment in your marketing department and the potential ROI on that investment.

To accomplish this, calculate the average cost of a salesperson. The following is a rough calculation of an average salesperson. Obviously, you will have to calculate costs from your own business model to determine an accurate ROI.

Marketing ROI Using a Salesperson Cost Example

The average base salary (or draw versus commission) for salespeople in our current economy ranges from $35,000 to $110,000 annually, depending on what they sell. In this example, I will use $87,500.

Salary	$87,500
Commissions calculated at quota	$100,000
Total annual compensation	$187,500
Plus benefits, taxes, insurance at 30% of labor cost	$56,250
Cost adding benefits and wages	$243,750
Travel and expenses calculated at $3,000/month	36,000
Total salesperson's annual cost	$279,750

For this example, the salesperson has a $1,500,000 annual quota and the firm operates on a service/product margin of 45%

Sales	$1,500,000
Minus cost of goods	$825,000

Total gross margin	$675,000
Total gross margin contribution before corporate G&A	$675,000
Minus total salesperson costs	$279,750
Equals gross revenue contribution per salesperson before corporate G&A (General and Administrative) costs	$395,250

This example is an estimate only. Your business may be different based on your model, market, sales overrides and corporate infrastructure costs. Additionally, this example does not calculate the cost of sales opportunities generated by the marketing department. This model assumes each salesperson will find, present and close all of his or her lead generation.

Using this example, you should generate $395,250 in gross revenue contribution before corporate G&A, or a **141% return on your investment** of $279,750 for the salesperson's cost.

With this number, you can now benchmark the marketing department's budget, with the assumption that it must return a minimum of 141% for every dollar invested.

Is this an accurate way to determine ROI for marketing projects? Yes and no.

The marketing department needs to understand that for every dollar they divert from the deployment of salespeople, they are potentially diverting a calculable

141% return on investment for the firm. Business development spending is based on maximizing revenue opportunities. Marketing departments, like other departments, must realize that all spending is tied to ROI.

When determining a budget value, you need to calculate its ROI potential against the same or greater investment in sales.

The Steps to Calculate Marketing ROI

1. Create or develop a twelve-month plan (month by month), listing each event or action the marketing department will take during the business fiscal year (i.e., September-seminar, direct mail and eZine; October-direct mail and Webinar).

2. Assign a fixed cost to each event based on the event's assigned budget.

3. Calculate the required ROI, in dollars, based on the event's contribution.

4. Verify that the project's ROI matches the ROI that a salesperson's costs would contribute.

5. Then, make a business decision. Is this an appropriate investment?

Measuring ROI Projects in Marketing

Marketing, to some degree, is the black hole that has never been held accountable to a measurable standard. As the position of marketing becomes more elevated, it is apparent that companies need to track the results of this department's actions as a business metric.

What kinds of metrics should you measure and what are their values?

Like our discussion on press and public relations (PR), there is vagueness to some ROI calculations when determining marketing programs. But, it behooves any senior management team to develop business measures.

The following can be directly measured in a price ratio:

- Direct mail
- Telemarketing
- Public seminars
- PR
- Webinars
- Print advertising
- Opt-in e-mail
- EZines
- Tradeshows

- Internal marketing material development

- Teleseminars

For example, if the cost of a direct mail lead is $100 and it takes twenty-five qualified leads to close a sale, then your marketing costs are $2,500 per order plus your marketing department overhead.

Spending business funds on branding, direct mail, websites, print ads, or electronic media advertisements is a waste of time and money if you cannot directly or indirectly trace these investments to lead generation or sales.

If you cannot track marketing ROI—then don't fund it.

Marketing managers and consultants love to talk about positional branding, image marketing, and viral communication. But, can any of these advisors help you confirm your marketing return on investment? No. They will tell you that you need to spend money to make money and that no visibility is no revenue. I agree with all of these statements but your marketing choices and delivery models must directly or indirectly generate revenue for you.

CEO SUCCESS ACTION STEPS

✓ If you don't already have marketing metrics in plan, set them up to measure your marketing program's performance. You will want to set up metrics for each marketing project.

✓ Review all marketing program expenditures for return on investment calculation.

Website_____

Tradeshow_____

Direct mail_____

Branding_____

Pay-Per-Click Advertising_____

Free Seminars/Workshops_____

E-mail and Electronic Newsletters_____

Print Ads_____

Social Networks_____

Other_____

✓ Evaluate whether you have project identifiers in place for each project so you can track the project's performance, i.e., sending prospects to a specific Web page that is only known by the prospects through a marketing piece such as a postcard and then enticing the prospect to take an action step to download a white paper.

✓ If you already have metrics in place, identify a marketing project that you can collect the metrics for and calculate the ROI for that project.

✓ Invest in marketing only when it generates prospect leads and its expenditure has a documentable return on investment. Determine your marketing cost per lead.

✓ Calculate how many leads it takes to make one sale.

Chapter 9

Develop a Replicable and Scalable Sales Process

To develop a replicable, scalable sales process that works with the majority of your sales team requires you to understand how and why your prospects buy. To accomplish this, you need to prototype your targeted and current buyers, evaluate your current sales process, and determine your sales goals by:

1. Understanding why prospects buy from you

2. Understanding why you lose business

3. Learning how to show "visual value" that buyers understand and believe

4. Documenting your sales process step-by-step

5. Quantifying your prospect prototype

6. Determining the fully loaded cost of one sale before corporate general and administrative (G & A) costs

7. Developing your sales metric benchmarks for success

8. Documenting your top ten sales objections with responses

9. Training your sales team regularly; role-playing often

10. Making cold calling to new prospects a requirement

11. Providing a market potential of at least 300 prospects per salesperson

12. Developing IT sales quotas that are accurate

13. Evaluating salespeople on metrics, not emotion

14. Assigning a maximum of three business industry verticals to each salesperson (preferably one)

15. Using lost sales analysis as a business tool

PROTOTYPING YOUR MOST LOGICAL IT BUYER

*"It's not what technology you built and who
you want to sell – it's who wants to buy!"*

CLIENT CASE STUDY

An IT staff aug and professional services company
headquartered in Boston, was seeking to expand its
selling market geography. They had some regional
success selling into Atlanta and estimated that to open
up a new branch office with programmers, salespeople,
recruiters, marketing, and admin would be at least $1
million the first year.

So, prior to making this investment, we did a market
demographic profile and success feasibility of their
business and found that their reasoning for going to
Atlanta was to create a new demand cycle for their
offerings. This $29 million company's current revenue
capture success had slowed to an annualized 4% during
the current economic environment. This was much
slower than the 16% growth per year they had for the
prior three years. They believed by "jumping" to a new
geography they would accelerate their growth curve
again.

But, after reviewing their revenue-capture model, we
found that they had over 3,900 new potential prospects
within a 150-mile radius of the corporate office that

they had never talked with. In fact, if they opened up their new office, their management team would drive by these prospects on the way to Logan Airport in Boston to catch their flight to Atlanta.

Prototyping buyers based on your value and their needs are a key driver to high tech success.

PROTOTYPING YOUR TARGETED PROSPECTS

Knowing your buyers is the key to selling more. Not knowing your buyers or their specific sales characteristics reduces your success. To prototype your buyer, research these areas:

- How does your product or service increase income, decrease expenses, or manage risks for the prospect?

- How does your product or service create value for the prospect?

- What are the business consequences if the prospect does not buy from you or another qualified vendor?

- What are the prospect titles that sign your contracts (VPs of Finance, VPs of Marketing, general managers, CEOs, etc.)?

- What is the average dollar value of your first sale to a prospect (by industry)?

- What are the top five business industries you sell into?

- What is the average annual revenue of the companies you sell to?

- What is your geographic selling zone (nationwide, local, etc.)?

- Calculate the average discount you give to a prospect—by title and industry.

- Calculate the average discount you give to a new prospect versus an existing customer.

- Determine the average length of time it takes to sell each prospect by title, industry, and buying option.

EVALUATING YOUR CURRENT IT SALES PROCESS

Knowing your current sales process will help you understand how your team currently operates, where the gaps are, and what is needed to build a replicable and scalable sales process. You will want to research these areas:

- What is the five-year value of a client after the first sale?

- Review all sales for the last 24 months and calculate your top ten accounts by revenue and what total percentages they contributed to overall corporate and department revenue.

- Review all sales staff success for the last 24 months and determine the percentage of success for sales to new prospects versus sales to existing customers (by individual salesperson and by the team as a whole).

- Determine the average sales experience, in years, of the top 10% of your sales team.

- Document the top ten sales objections your sales team hears from prospects by title, industry, and annual revenue.

- Determine what questioning techniques your sales team currently uses to determine when a prospect is a qualified buyer.

- Based on your sales success, determine the method used to generate leads that resulted in closed deals during the last 24 months (cold calling, networking, marketing, etc.).

- Review all of your sales during the last 24 months and determine what percentage of deals required your management team to meet with the prospect to close the business.

- Ascertain and document the steps needed to close an IT product or service sale (cold call, first meeting, discovery meeting, presentation, proposal development, proposal submittal, etc.).

- Determine the cost for each lead provided to your sales team (total corporate new revenue generated for one year divided by total number of leads generated by marketing = cost per lead).

DETERMINING YOUR SALES GOALS

Current sales models and prototype buyers may not be the targeted prospects your salespeople are seeking to sell. At times, salespeople take the path of least resistance and sell to prospects they feel comfortable selling to, not necessarily who you, as management, want them to sell.

To develop your structured sales process, you must measure the gap between your current sales model, your current prospect prototype, and your corporate selling goals. If there is no gap, then (and only then) you can develop your sales process.

If there is a gap between your current corporate objectives and your sales team's actions, you must reduce the gap to help your sales team focus on the company's needs—not their needs.

- Is your sales team selling to the targeted prospects you wish them to sell?

- Does your sales team focus on the right prospect title?

- Is your sales team only selling to existing customers?

With the data from these questions, you can develop and write your sales process.

PULLING IT ALL TOGETHER AND DOCUMENTING YOUR SALES PROCESS

Once you have prototyped your targeted prospects and current sales model, you can now integrate these two resources into a written sales process that helps your sales team understand your model and the expectations you have for them to sell. Your sales process is the framework from which you and your sales team both operate and it should be in a written format. Once the sales process is documented, it should be used as a tool to teach and manage your sales team. Your sales process must:

- Describe who your targeted industries are and what their annual revenues are.

- Identify the title of the targeted prospect.

- Describe the IT products and services you expect your sales team to sell.

- Describe the targeted average price per sale for each product and service you sell (gross profit or gross margin).

- Describe the anticipated sales objections the sales rep can expect to hear from each industry they sell to and from each prospect title they are expected to sell.

- List each sales step expected for each product and service you sell.

- List how your sales team must qualify prospects at each sales step to determine if they should continue working with the prospect.

- Identify the anticipated length of time it should take to close a sale from beginning to end.

- Identify sales metric benchmarks for success.

- Determine the expectations of lead generation (i.e., cold calling, networking, marketing, etc.).

- Describe when and how often the company will provide sales training.

Once you have gathered this information, pull it in a written document that you can provide to your sales team, and as needed, to your management team. You should review your sales process twice a year to make sure it is relevant to the current selling environment you operate in.

CEO SUCCESS ACTION STEPS

✓ Complete all of the questions in this chapter. Develop, revise, and adjust a new, detailed, written sales process for your firm based on the core competence of your firm specifically.

✓ Implement a written sales process for your team based on the criteria discussed in this chapter.

Chapter 10

Manage Your Sales Process and Sales Quotas Through a Premeditated Approach

Sales forecasting is a key business driver

You could make a case that the reason Enron Corporation was forced into bankruptcy is because their sales forecasts were wrong. Up until the year 2000, Enron was deep into buying companies in a classic roll-up market move. Like all public companies, their revenue forecasts were diligently followed by Wall Street analysts. As soon as they missed their numbers, internally the accounting and finance departments started looking for ways to drop the company breakeven and corporate G & A costs. During this exposition, one of their managers uncovered the fraud and corruption that had been taking place and the rest is history.

But, what if the company's sales forecasts were accurate? Their stock would have gone up, Wall Street and Enron's investors would have been happy, and their executive shenanigans (which have been going on in Global 1000 company's corner offices for 100 years) would have been buried in four-point font in the back of the firm's 10 K report.

Sales forecasts are the foundational metric to run your company. In IT, it is even more important. Bench utilization rates, hardware purchases, marketing budget allocations, installation time tables, client training schedules, and corporate cash flow are all tied to sales forecast accuracy.

Accurate sales forecasts are achieved by calculating IT sales quotas correctly using a structured approach.

Creating a Sales Forecast

Sales forecasting is part art, part human perception, and part sales management metrics.

Salespeople need to find prospects that will take action steps with them during the sales cycle to prove they should continue to work with them. This method of sales is called **transactional selling**. Most of the time, salespeople talk about relationship selling and insert their "relationships" into the sales forecasts without any business logic other than their perception of the buyer's interaction with them.

In fact, many times relationship selling starts after the second sale.

Why? Because, when you talk about having a relationship with the prospect, you are not talking about how often they talk with you, meet with you, or respond to your e-mails. Relationship selling happens *after* the prospect has bought at least once from you, so they can determine if the value they received in the post-sales transaction is what you said would be delivered to them during the pre-sales discussions. It is during the post-sale that a buyer makes a judgment call and decides to have a business relationship with you by buying a second time.

So, when building out your sales forecasts, do not let salespeople build their forecast based on their perception of the prospects' needs (their relationships). Often salespeople will "rainbow" their sales forecasts by projecting their needs onto the buyer rather than the actual action steps taken by the prospect towards an acquisition.

Accurate sales forecasts are crucial to company success. When you have an accurate sales forecast (over 80% accuracy), you can take it to the bank and get a line of credit. Sales forecasts drive your company's cash flow, staffing requirements, engineering needs, and marketing budget. When your sales forecast is incorrect, your entire department or company is affected.

As stated, a sales forecast is a snapshot of time that changes every day. To help manage the human emotion of sales forecasting by salespeople, you must use specific, quantifiable benchmarks to document transactional sales steps and measure sales forecasting accuracy.

Salespeople, by their very nature, are overly optimistic, so you need to manage their enthusiasm with a quantitative approach. For sales opportunities to be placed into a 90-day sales forecast, the account manager must be able to answer these questions correctly for you.

1. Does the prospect have a budget for your product or service? If so, how much?

2. Who is making the decision to buy?

3. Who is signing the purchase order or contract?

4. Who else will be involved in this decision (managers, steering committee, etc.)?

5. When does the prospect want to have this product or service (operational, installed, bought, and launched, in inventory, etc.)?

6. How will this purchase help the prospect's firm?

7. What will be the prospect's business consequences if they don't buy at all or if they

buy from the wrong vendor? (This is called consequence management.)

If your salesperson cannot answer these questions correctly, never insert the sales opportunity into their sales forecast.

Some of your sales team will want to move their pipeline opportunities into their sales forecasts without answering all of these questions . . . but don't let them. By using this method, you will clean up the accuracy of your forecasts, while putting pressure on your sales team to move prospects from a sales pipeline opportunity into a qualified sales forecast opportunity.

When setting up your forecasts, you want to use a sales process that identifies action steps, thereby forcing your sales team members to quantify where they are in their sales metrics for each prospect opportunity.

1. Sales forecasts should be supplied by all salespeople at least monthly; but preferably weekly.

2. The sales forecast should be set up on 30-day, 60-day, and 90-day time lines. This is designed to identify sales closing barriers, a salesperson's progress, revenue projects, and business cash flow. By assigning a date (within 90 days) and a sales step approach, you are managing sales team members' inaccurate perceptions of where they think they are in the sales cycle.

3. All sales forecasts should be taken by management directly from a contact manager or Customer Relations Manager (CRM) system each Friday by 12:00 noon based on business deals with a 70% or higher probability of closing and <u>list the month they are anticipated to close.</u>

4. All information inserted in the contact manager/CRM after 12:00 noon each Friday will not be included in the Monday sales meeting forecast and will be posted to the following Friday's sales forecast.

NOTE: It is the responsibility of each employee (not the sales manager) who handles direct sales, partner sales, or renewal sales to insert updated prospect information and sales cycle probability in the contact manager/CRM on a daily basis.

Tightening the Sales Forecast

All accounts should be entered into the contact manager/CRM in the opportunity section, with the following probability percentages based on these sales steps and the projected close date.

100%   A signed agreement or purchase order has been received.

90%   Contract terms are being reviewed by the prospect's legal department or being negotiated.

80%   A verbal order where the paperwork will be done within 2 weeks, and the proposal and contracts have been submitted.

70%   The deal should be yours, but your competition is still present.

Differentiating Between a Forecast and a Pipeline

A **sales forecast** contains all prospects projected to be closed within 90 days that have an opportunity code of 70% or higher and meet the following qualifying questions:

1. The person you are working with is the decision maker and is signing the purchase order or contract.

2. The person you are working with has stated a budget and your product or service offering falls within the range of that stated budget.

3. The decision maker has told you that she will be buying a product or service like yours within 90 days.

A **sales pipeline** contains all prospects that have less than a 70% probability and will not be closed within 90 days. These should be inserted into the opportunity field with one of the following percentages and an estimated date to close.

60%	Active deal–competition is equal.
50%	Active deal this calendar year.
40%-10%	Prospective deals that may happen this calendar year.

Sales Forecast Example:

A product or service deal expected to be closed within 90 days, during the month of June, where you *should* win, but there is competition present, would be coded as "June 70%."

This approach of a metric-driven sales forecast based on sales steps tied to dates helps control the common problem many sales managers have called "sales projection." Sales projection is when sales team members "project" their needs—to sell, to increase their commissions, to hit their sales quotas, and in some cases, to keep their jobs—onto buyers. By packaging the sales forecast into quantitative sales steps, you minimize sales projection and increase the efficiency of your sales team.

You can use this basic format or develop your own based on the sales step requirements you have for an average product or service sale within your company.

The key to setting up a metric-based sales forecasting program is **tying the sales steps to time**.

COMMON QUOTA CALCULATION MISTAKES

Often IT sales quotas are calculated based on some arbitrary corporate goal for revenue enlargement rather than on business metrics. For example, at one company I consulted with, a mid-sized professional services and project management firm, the Vice President of Operations and the CFO determined the sales quotas for the sales force. The VP calculated his department's overhead, added a 40% gross margin to that number, and this became the sales department's annual goal. He then took this number and divided it by the number of salespeople he thought they needed.

Voila! Like magic, they had a sales quota for the sales team.

This impractical and unscientific sales quota determination happens time and time again. More often than not, the sales quota is based on commitments to investors, family owners, bankers, stockholders, or just aggressive business goals, combined with the accounting department's perception of what the cost of sales should be.

The short-term losers are the sales reps as they struggle to make their monthly numbers.

The long-term losers are the company's affiliated departments because they have built their business models based on a fabricated sales quota.

Here are the top ten most common methods technology firms use to *miscalculate* their sales quotas:

- An increase percentage-wise over last year's territory sales numbers

- The cost of the salesperson times a multiplier (salesperson's cost x 3)

- The cost of corporate General and Administrative (G & A) overhead plus an arbitrary gross margin added in

- Total company revenue goals committed to Wall Street or investors divided by the number of salespeople in the company

- The total revenue goal of the Vice President of Sales divided by the number of salespeople

- A sales quota designed to support an imaginary compensation plan that was sold to the salesperson as his income potential if he hit 100% quota

- What an industry's trade press says is the annual growth rate this year for your market (growth up 12%, quotas are up 12%)

- The Vice President of Sales' quota experiences at other companies

- A salesperson's success from the previous year in her territory (quota is 110% of last year's sales)

- A percentage of what the top salesperson did last year in her territory (90% of what the top salesperson sold last year)

Are any of these methods used by your firm to calculate sales quotas?

How do these sales quota calculation methods support the potential of a particular salesperson's territory? These measurements are based on outside influences and expenses, which are completely unrelated to the sales and market potential of the product or service in an assigned territory and the ability of a salesperson to hit it.

The fact is: none of these methods are accurate.

These impractical and unscientific sales quota determination methods just frustrate everyone. When they are wrong, they affect the whole company. The operations and engineering departments become frustrated because their capacity usage is low and they end up blaming the sales department because they haven't hit their numbers. The accounting department becomes irritated because accounts receivables are shrinking, and investors are frustrated because their financial milestones are missed.

Are these elements important in determining your company's costs and revenue opportunities? Yes, of course; but if the approach for sales quota (or target) is backwards, then the poor results it gets should be expected.

103

CALCULATING IT SALES QUOTAS CORRECTLY

To forecast sales goals correctly, don't determine what sales should do based on company needs. Determine what the sales department **can do based on the market opportunity and the sales model success your firm uses**. From that calculation, you can determine what other departments' overhead should be, as well as corporate G & A, to build your sales forecast.

Below is a more accurate (and simplified) sales quota determination method:

First, determine what the true sales potential is for your IT product or service from each salesperson's territory, city by city and industry by industry. Determine the potential dollar size for one year of sales within the market segment or geography in which your product or service salespeople are assigned. This market potential is the *total sales potential for the market*, not just what you can sell. Quotas do not have to be equal by sales account representative or by territory. Your marketing department should provide this information to you, or you need to calculate this yourself.

Then, look at the length of time in months it takes for a sales lead to be generated and the number of leads needed to generate one prospect proposal. You will need sales metrics in order to determine this. If you don't have metrics in place, start collecting them.

Next, look at the average value in dollars of each IT product or service you sell.

Then, determine what the average closing ratio is for all salespeople for each IT product and service you sell. This figure is based on number of deals proposed versus number of deals actually closed. For example, if a salesperson closes one out of every four deals his closing ratio is 25%.

Last, determine the number of potential prospect leads needed to generate one qualified proposal.

With this data, you can now determine what each salesperson's target quota should be. Let's use this simple formula to calculate an example quota.

Sales Quota Calculation Example and Formula:

Sales Quota = Territory potential (÷) average sale in dollars (÷) number of leads needed to generate a proposal (x) average closing ratio (x) average value of one deal.

Facts and Stats
Territory potential $10,000,000

Average sales value $300,000

> *Calculation*
> Territory potential divided by average sale in dollars equals potential number of sales in units.
>
> $10,000,000 ÷ $300,000 = 33.3 sales lead potential in the territory

Facts and Stats
Number of potential unit sales in the territory 33.3

Number of leads needed to generate one proposal 4

> *Calculation*
> Number of territory potential unit sales divided by the
> number of leads needed to generate a proposal equals
> the number of potential deals per year.
>
> 33.3 ÷ 4 = 8.325 potential deals this year in this territory

Facts and Stats
Number of potential deals 8.325

Average company closing ratio
for this product or service 25%

> *Calculation*
> Number of potential deals multiplied by closing ratio
> equals number of actual deals sold in a territory per year.
>
> 8.325 x 25% = 2.08 deals sold in territory

Facts and Stats
Actual deals sold per year 2.08

Average dollar value per deal $300,000

> *Calculation*
> Number of actual deals multiplied by the average value
> per deal equals the annual sales quota.
>
> 2.08 x $300,000 = $624,000

Summary of Facts and Stats
Territory Potential $10,000,000

Average dollar value per deal $300,000

Number of potential unit sales in the territory 33.3

Number of leads needed to generate one proposal 4

Number of potential deals 8.325

Average company closing ratio 25%

Actual deals sold per year 2.08

Actual quota dollars per year $624,000

Average time to close a deal .... 6 months

Using this formula, you are going to find that many sales quotas are inflated and not based on actual potential or reality.

Is this a simplistic formula? *Yes.*

Does it take into consideration add-on sales for existing clients, new product introductions, or one-time large sales anomalies? *No.*

Can these numbers be improved by adjusting the closing ratios or the leads-to-proposal success factor? *Yes.*

These are key factors that can increase a sales rep's success and quota assignments without adjusting market size. From this sales quota calculation, you now have a benchmark that can be backed into operational delivery costs, salesperson compensation, and G & A costs to determine the corporate financial needs and revenue goals.

Does this take work? *Yes.*

Can you do it for a national sales force with 200+ account sales reps? *Absolutely.*

It is difficult to understand why so many firms generate sales forecasts based on incorrect variables and then carry the miscalculations forward. It is better to have your marketing department spend three months determining the real potential of each sales rep's territory than to guess and have all corporate budgets wrong.

As a senior executive, you need to maximize your sales team's ability to increase revenue. Increased revenue is centered on the ability to improve closing ratios, increase lead generation, maximize human capital capabilities, and forecast correctly. An accurate sales quota is the first step to managing the sales team's success.

Factors That Affect an IT Salesperson's Performance

Although there are many factors that can influence whether a salesperson hits her sales quota, I have found there are 20 consistent factors that appear regularly:

SALES SKILLS AFFECTING SALES QUOTA SUCCESS

- The salesperson's lack of personal initiative.

- The salesperson's poor understanding of the client's operational needs and their inability to describe how your IT offerings can fix their business problems.

- The salesperson's inability to discuss her product or service offering in detail.

- Minimal cold call efforts by the salesperson.

- The salesperson's lack of presentation skills.

- The salesperson's lack of prospect negotiation skills.

- The salesperson's inability to read sales cycle signs with the prospect.

- Poor time management by the salesperson.

MANAGEMENT SKILLS AFFECTING SALES QUOTA SUCCESS

- Poor management advice on account sales techniques.

- Lack of positive motivational advice to the salesperson.

- Management interference in account sales relationships.

- Lack of product or service training supplied on a regular basis.

- Lack of sales training supplied on a regular basis.

- Incorrect sales quota calculation.

- Lack of sales training that teaches account managers how to be business success advisors.

COMPANY ISSUES AFFECTING SALES QUOTA SUCCESS

- The IT product or service offering is not competitive.

- The company has poor customer service and/or support.

- The market demand for the product or service is decreasing.

- The product or service does not work as marketed (lots of software bugs …).

- The compensation plan is incorrect and does not drive the salesperson's performance.

All but one of these factors can be controlled through corporate training, market research, and adjustments to the sales process. It is the first one—personal initiative—that is outside the control of the company.

CASE STUDY

A West Coast public IT company whose direct sales team sells enterprise application to distributors came to me because one of its operating business divisions that focused on the small to medium market (SMB) was losing money. It seemed that their sales and marketing expenses were disproportionate to their customer lifetime value. Additionally, they had a large turnover in their sales team because none of the team members were making enough money to warrant the labor it took to sell their targeted prospects.

After we analyzed their software application offerings, sales team metrics, marketing communication and methods, strategy approach, and their team's selling process, we discovered that it took the average salesperson seven on-site meetings to close one deal that was worth $28,000. Each salesperson was being paid a $50,000 base salary and between 6-10% of gross revenue of each sale and had a sales quota of $600,000. From proposals submitted, the sales team had an average closing ratio of 22% or about one out of five clients. That meant their average selling cycle to close one deal was five customers with seven on-site meetings—or thirty-five onsite meetings in total. There are only 200 business selling days a year when you count buyer vacations, weekends, and holidays. So the average salesperson was selling five to six deals a year for a total of $170,000 a year or 34% of their assigned quota.

After the initial sale was made, the prospect lifetime value contribution was less than $100,000 over ten years.

Their business unit (BU) did not use an integrated revenue capture process. Their divisional profitability was affected because multiple departments, including marketing, sales, corporate strategy, application pricing, and technology development were all operating as silos not relevant to buyer requirements needed to make their operating unit model successful. So, once we had completed our 360° Success Assessment and Recommendation Program we found the software was too sophisticated for the average buyer and its price was too low based on the value it produced for a buyer who understood its capabilities. This forced the sales team to keep going back to the same targeted buyer to "demo" again and again to try to sell the over-developed app to a buyer who did not understand what he was buying and thought it was too much money!

So, I suggested that they carve up the application into a light version that could be sold for $10,000 long distance, over the telephone and through webinars, over two years to the prospect, in module-by-module upgrades.

Then we took the current sophisticated app and moved its price point up to a minimum of $100,000 and set up a national sales pursuit team model to go after the identified largest 1000 prospects through a direct sales channel. For buyers in the $25,000 to $100,000 price point range, we set up a national VAR program and signed 157 channel partners over the first six months.

Today, the division is growing year over year in profitability and top-line revenues.

Developing a successful, replicable, and measurable sales process is one element of growing your firm. The correct sales process should increase corporate profitability and minimize and eliminate business errors that reduce your sales operational efficiencies. Successful sales processes are roadmaps that can be used by a broad range of sales team members over and over again. They pull up the skills of average salespeople to a corporate minimum, while helping senior salespeople expand their achievements.

Deploying and managing sales metrics is an integral part of successful management. Sales processes driven by metrics allow you to:

- Reduce your sales cycle time to close the deal

- Reduce sales capture costs per sale, including travel and expenses

- Increase your sales team's success

- Develop a training program based on factual sales needs

- Increase your sales team retention

- Increase the efficiencies of your operations, engineering, and R&D departments

IT companies generally fall into one of four sales process categories:

1. A sales process based on other companies' business practices

2. A sales process based on unsubstantiated sales successes

3. A sales process based on one salesperson's success or the selling experiences of the founder or senior manager

4. No written sales process exists at all

Each of these methods will hinder your ability to manage salespeople and deploy a scalable and replicable sales process. Let's take a closer look.

A sales process based on other companies' business practices.

Many times, a company will look at the sales processes of its competitors or those described in industry trade publications as models to emulate. They assume by this method of imitation that their firm will have the same success as these other companies. But, generally, this doesn't work because each company's product and service strengths and weaknesses are uniquely different. Additionally, the sales team competence may not be the same. For example, having a $20 million company adjust its sales process to match that of a Fortune 1000 company usually fails because the sales process of a Fortune 1000 company is not designed for revenue capture, it is designed for discipline and control.

A sales process based on unsubstantiated sales successes.

For a sales process to work, it must be based on substantiated and documented successful sales steps and buyer profiling to maximize its effectiveness.

A sales process based on one salesperson's success or the selling experiences of the founder or senior manager.

Just because one salesperson, or the founder of the company, has been successful selling the company's product or service, does not mean that their sales process is scalable or replicable for the average salesperson.

No written sales process exists at all.

Today, many firms use a verbalized sales process or an implied sales process, rather than having a premeditated, documented selling process for their sales team that can be replicated on an ongoing basis.

Often, sales methodology in many companies becomes a haphazard approach, where some people sell and others don't. As I mentioned earlier, part of the reason this occurs is because many sales processes are carried over from company to company without consideration for size, product, service, sales force, or management team. This haphazard approach exists throughout the entire world, in big companies and small, start-ups and mature players. A written sales process is the framework of sales success.

CEO SUCCESS ACTION STEPS

✓ As you develop your written step-by-step sales process from the previous chapter, outline the number of on-site client meetings, webinars, and prospect interactions that are needed to sell one deal based on its dollar value.

✓ Focus on calculating sales quotas mathematically.

✓ Try to minimize roadblocks to salesperson success.

Chapter 11

Manage Your Prospects and Existing Customer Base Profitably—Or They Will Close Your Doors For You

It is not *customers*—it is *gross revenue*. Better yet, it's not *gross revenue*—it is *profit*.

D o your company's technology and professional services have value? Do your business offerings help your customers (buyers) increase their business income, decrease expenses, or manage business risks and consequences? Of course, they do.

Yet many IT management team members act subservient to their customers and clients and perform as indentured servants who are not allowed to raise prices and must give continuous freebies whenever there is a request.

117

When customers buy from you on a regular basis, it should communicate to you that the buyer has identified that your offerings have a **stated value that is greater than the risks they would have when buying from a new vendor**.

When managing existing customers' profitably remember these three theorems:

- Customers know your value; prospects don't!

- Price must equal value—when it doesn't, then your price is too high!

- It is not what your offering costs you, but what it is worth to the buyer.

Why do management teams give the greatest price discounts to existing customers who already know their value? Usually it is a strategic reaction because management has no choice and must be obedient servants to their clients to maintain the firm's current cash flow. This customer price discounting is often a reflection of the firm's weak outbound marketing and sales process.

Oftentimes your competition for existing customers to buy your offering again is not competitors in your market place; rather it is the lack of action by the customer to buy anything or their comparison of your investment cost and value to another investment cost and value not related to what you sell.

As the CEO, you need to maximize your firm's existing-customer value by communicating to them specifically why they need to buy from you on a regular basis. In my book, *HOW TO SELL TECHNOLOGY*, this communication process is called "being professionally blunt." Not rude or disrespectful, but peer-to-peer interaction, where you become a strategic advisor who tells them the truth.

If you want to be a strategic advisor to your customers and you believe that your IT product or service is a tool to help them increase income, decrease expenses, or manage business risks or consequences, then you have a fiduciary responsibility to tell them directly.

Remember, customers and prospects do not always know how to buy correctly.

What happens in most sales paradigms is that all prospects, regardless of the offering price, make a pre-sales assumption of their purchase value. Then they buy. Once the purchase is completed, they go through a post-sales analysis of what they bought and make a calculation of their purchase value to confirm or deny you sold them the value they perceived they would get during the pre-sales analysis. If they did receive the value perceived, then they have a greater risk of going with a new untested vendor in the future.

When your existing customers are getting the value they sought, you need to raise their pricing on a regular basis. If you truly offer great value to your current IT customers, it is a greater risk for them to buy from another vendor than to buy from you because you raised your prices 4% this year.

Managing Technology Buyers Who Do Not Know How to Buy Correctly

One mistake often made when developing IT marketing strategies is the belief that the targeted prospect knows how to buy your technology or professional service offerings correctly.

This assumption is either based on the seniority of the title of the targeted prospect companies you are trying to sell or how often the prospect has actually bought your type of offering before, i.e., previous buying experience means they know what they are doing. Realize it is not uncommon for "experienced buyers" to buy incorrectly over and over again. And when prospects do make incorrect buying decisions, they may not have funding to correct the wrong purchase for years, so they live with the mistake and you live with the lost revenue.

Never assume that prospects know what they are doing, no matter what the title of the buyer is or the verbose declarations they give you on how broad their experience level is in acquiring the IT you sell. To increase the communication and understanding of the value of what you sell, you must always assume that targeted prospects do not know how to buy your IT offering correctly.

To manage their information gap, send a continuous flow of education and thought-leadership marketing devices that force prospects to become knowledgeable and subliminally teaches them how to buy and what to buy from you.

One success tool to use is a whitepaper approach entitled "10 Questions You Should Ask Before You Buy" which is handed out to target prospects to force them to learn how to buy your IT offering correctly.

Is this a cynical approach to marketing to customers? No, because it minimizes the knowledge gap of what you know and what they know and increases their retention through repetition. Certainly knowledge is not the only driver that forces correct buying practices— but it does reduce acquisition error.

CASE STUDY

In 2002, I was interviewed by Gerry Gregoire, an editor of CIO Magazine. Gerry is the former CIO of Dell Computer and Pepsi-Cola Worldwide. During our conversations, Gerry mentioned that in my book *How To Sell Technology*, I left out a critical chapter on why technology salespeople need to be more ethical and not sell vaporware.

I responded that although there are unprincipled salespeople who misrepresent their technology and professional service capabilities and delivery potential to get the sale they were the exception and not the rule.

I told him that IT salespeople don't go into the backroom, make up the proposal and their IT offering deliverables in a vacuum and just submit it to a buyer. But, in fact most proposals (especially large proposals for Global 1000 firms like his) are a collaborative process where the VP of Operations reviews the specifications, the VP of Finance reviews the costs, and the VP of Sales and sometimes the CEO, depending on the deal size, determine the price point to sell at.

In fact, many times IT salespeople are just business liaisons delivering the proposal for the company as a whole. So, if the technology doesn't work the reasons are usually more than just the sales team member's fault and in fact could be many company issues. "But," I also added, "for technology acquisitions to be successful, there is a fiduciary responsibility for the buyer to know what they are buying, to perform due diligence on references, and to assign a competent, prepared project manager."

The salient point of his comment, is that if a CIO of a Global 1000 firm, can't buy an IT purchase correctly using all of the resources he has available, including legal departments, administration, technical analysts, and legions of support team members, then IT sales organizations cannot rely on the perceived knowledge of the buyer.

Let's be honest, most IT buyers don't know how to buy correctly, regardless of their education, positional authority, or past purchase experiences. They could have bought a CRM system five times during the last fifteen years and bought it wrong every time.

So, to increase marketing ROI, focus on educating buyers on how to buy your offering properly, not just why they should buy what you are offering.

CEO SUCCESS ACTION STEPS

✓ Determine the value you give to prospects, communicate it often, and raise your pricing to them on a regular basis.

✓ Calculate the value of each product and service you sell. Develop a schedule to raise pricing.

✓ Create sales objection whitepapers that educate prospects on how to buy correctly.

Chapter 12

Focus On Your Customers' Lifetime Value to Grow Your Business

C ustomer value is not a short-term calculation. When marketing, selling, and servicing IT clients, one of the largest overhead areas for most firms is their sales and marketing costs.

One way to manage this expenditure is to build a premeditated client lifetime value model that tracks total customer value over a predetermined timeline. Understating a customer's gross revenue and cost expense impacts your business throughout the entire buying cycle. And, having this data will help you price your offering both on the first sale and subsequent orders.

Caution: only focusing on sales to existing clients will diminish your firm's potential for consistent top-line revenue growth.

Sales-Revenue Capture Value Test

1. Does your firm get asked to drop its price more than 50% of the time by prospects before they will buy?

   ☐ Yes   ☐ No

2. When you lose a deal, do prospects tell you more than 50% of the time that your price was too high?

   ☐ Yes   ☐ No

3. Do you sell your firm's product or service horizontally to everyone or do you sell vertically to specific markets?

   ☐ Horizontally   ☐ Vertically

4. Does your firm lead with price as its value proposition when presenting to a prospect?

   ☐ Yes   ☐ No

5. In order to close a deal, does your sales team have a standard price discount they are allowed to give to a prospect without management approval?

   ☐ Yes   ☐ No

6. Is your sales staff paid on gross margin or gross revenue?

   ☐ Gross Margin   ☐ Gross Revenue

7. Is the word "price" mentioned anywhere in your advertising, including in sales brochures, letters to prospects, or your website?

   ☐ Yes   ☐ No

8. In the final sales-cycle steps, after seeing your proposal and talking with your competitors, do clients ask you to explain how you are different more than 50% of the time?

   ☐ Yes   ☐ No

9. Are your pricing metrics based on your competitors' prices?

   ☐ Yes   ☐ No

10. On repeat sales to existing clients, do your clients hold you hostage for discounts to get add-on business?

    ☐ Yes   ☐ No

ANSWERS

1. No	5. No	9. No
2. No	6. Gross margin	10. No

3. Vertically   7. No
4. No   8. No

SCORING

Each correct answer is worth 10 points. Each incorrect answer is worth 0 points. Add up your score. The higher your score the greater your understanding of how your buyers see and believe your value.

When setting up a revenue-capture program, your goals should be to:

- Capture 50% of revenue from existing customers

- Capture 50% of revenue from new customers

Why? Because when revenue-capture goals are totally dependent on selling new business only to existing customers, you minimize your company's long-term growth based on your current customers' ability to buy now. At times, your current customers can't buy. So, a more structured program seeks a balanced revenue-capture process that focuses equally on new business from new prospects and new business from existing customers.

Another successful revenue-capture program geared to existing clients is the **Value Forward 5-Year Revenue Replacement Model**. This is a planned process where management teams build profit centers for a customer based on the first sale and projected future sales over a five-year timeline.

The 5-year revenue replacement model guidelines are:

- Each customer you sell should generate a minimum of 2x (two times the original value) in add-on revenue streams over the next three to five years.

- For every new company you sell, plot out a 36- to 60-month timeline of new services and programs that you can sell back to them.

- Create new technology and professional services that can be up-sold and cross-sold.

- Dedicate salespeople to focus on existing client sales only.

EXAMPLE

1st Client Sale - Software	$100,000
1st Year Revenue Replacement Goal	$33,000
2nd Year Revenue Replacement Goal	$33,000
3rd Year Revenue Replacement Goal	$33,000
4th Year Revenue Replacement Goal	$33,000
5th Year Revenue Replacement Goal	$33,000

1st Year Add-on

A/R Accounting Module	$10,000
New-User Training	$5,000
Increase in Maintenance Support Agreement	$1,000
Custom Development	$15,000
Special Report Created	<u>$2,000</u>
Total	$33,000

Most company's look at client lifetime values as an incremental and unplanned process, either because the company doesn't have additional technology and professional services to sell or they just assume existing customers will buy more from them.

Revenue capture should never be an unplanned process and should be linked to a strategy. Remember, prospects are not loyal and customers are barely loyal.

Every strategic action must have a tactical action linked to it so use revenue replacement models as a planned approach. Throughout this book, we consistently move backward and forward between strategic and tactical actions. Yet in all cases, they need to be linked together.

Here are 5 steps to grow your business using a strategic and tactical action linkage model.

5 Action Steps to Grow Your Company

1. Standardize Your Business Process

   o **Strategic Action:** Prepare detailed P&L statements for every department. Although many firms have generic P&L statements, the more segmented the P&L statements are by department, the more accurate the information is for the CEO to make business decisions on, i.e., where to invest in order to grow the firm.

   o **Tactical Action:** Manage all departments based on predetermined department business metrics where all department practices are benchmarked.

2. Prepare a Market Gap Analysis

   o **Strategic Action:** Calculate your market demand based on research, not collective assumptions.

   o **Tactical Action:** Determine objective reasons why prospects will buy from you and not your competitors.

3. Develop Product/Service Competence

   o **Strategic Action:** Have a core strength based on your intellectual property to differentiate yourself from competitors.

o **Tactical Action:** Continually reinvest in your intellectual property (service, support, or applications, etc.) to maintain your intellectual property strengths.

4. Identify Revenue Impediments

o **Strategic Action:** Management must be business-mature to "see" when problems exist.

o **Tactical Action:** When revenue impediments are identified, management must be able to respond with corrective action steps to resolve these business issues.

5. Deploy a Documented Sales Process Based on Outbound Hunting for New Business

6. **Strategic Action:** Focus corporate sales strategies on harvesting revenue from new accounts as well as existing customers.

7. **Tactical Action:** Sales programs must be designed to allow growth to happen by creating replicable sales model procedures that can be duplicated by all salespeople and which are not single sales anomalies.

CEO SUCCESS ACTION STEPS

✓ Set up a Revenue Replacement Model for your company.

✓ Make a list of new technology and professional services you will sell over a specific timeline to each prospect using a premeditated format.

✓ Adjust your sales team's compensation to increase business from new prospects.

✓ Build linkage between both strategic and tactical action steps to improve your operational performance.

Chapter 13

Make Customer Service a Profit Center

How often have you been left on hold or had a customer service rep act like his brain was somewhere in another universe when you were trying to explain a billing error? Today, as companies try to reduce their operating costs by outsourcing customer service overseas, customer service is an oxymoron.

You and I are buyers and daily we subliminally judge our vendor relationships based on past experiences and expectations of what we believe is the acceptable support standard that we deserve.

This customer service expectation extends to technical support, salespeople, management, secretaries, delivery staff, and loading dock members—basically all employees who interact with customers and buyers during the pre-sales, sales, and post-sales interactions.

When managed proactively, customer service can be a valuable business asset that can increase corporate-revenue capture. Ignore it, and you will waste your marketing and advertising investments and brand-building message.

Customer service should be structured as a profit center, not as an expense center. This takes a proactive commitment by the CEO who understands that **any exposure to an existing customer and/or new prospect is an opportunity to increase revenue**.

8 Ways to Use IT Customer Service to Increase Revenue

1. Realize that every person in your company will have the opportunity to interact with your customers. All it takes is one employee to incorrectly handle a prospect or customer interaction and your business loses revenue. Develop a company Communication Handbook and train all employees on what is appropriate customer service interaction.

2. Create specific technology and professional services to be marketed **only** by the customer service department team members so that all of your revenue-capture options are extended over a broader line of customer-facing employees.

3. Train customer service account managers on how to support inbound calls in a positive manner and how to sell your offerings.

4. Develop a cross-sell and up-sell option handout for all of your team members so they can identify selling opportunities when they happen.

5. Create a list of circumstances when a specific customer service offering should be presented to a new prospect or an existing customer. Use this list as a marketing tool for customer service representatives.

6. When developing new or updating old IT offerings, name the customer service program based on the goal of your sale, not some techie name (i.e., The Client New Business Launch Program, The Customer Appreciation Program, The New Employee Training Enhancement Program, The Cost Containment Program, etc.).

7. If the support representative is not in a position to cross-sell or up-sell a customer directly (because the product or service you sell is too complex), create a "spiff bonus" for the support representative or the department based on new sales from existing customers that they directly or indirectly handle.

8. Assign financial goals (objectives, sales quotas, etc.) independent of the sales team to the customer service department. Give bonuses or department awards when these objectives are reached. Treat customer service as a standalone profit center.

CEO SUCCESS ACTION STEPS

✓ Move customer service from an expense center to a profit center.

✓ Develop tools to enable customer service to successfully sell to new and existing customers.

✓ Name your IT offerings based on the value it creates for your targeted buyer.

Chapter 14

Use Strategic Alliances and Channel Partners to Increase Revenue

Another best-practices process we have observed with successful IT companies is partnering more, not less, with other successful companies.

Strategic alliances are an important business asset tool, which allows CEOs to leverage their corporate assets and resources with other firms to enlarge their market penetration and increase corporate-revenue capture. Often CEOs become proprietary and ethnocentric in their thinking when considering using the concept of business leverage and they bypass this option because they believe their core competence is unique to them. This is a mistake.

I remember when I was a little boy, my grandfather, a successful entrepreneur from Sicily with only a fifth-grade education, telling me that to expand your business, you must go beyond using family members and seek out others who can help you grow your company—analytical thinking from a street-trained mogul.

Yet, how often do private family-run businesses not expand because they don't trust "outsiders?" This hesitation to work with others forces the company to maximize its growth potential only through the use of its own assets and knowledge center, which usually limits long-term growth.

Like the real estate industry concept of OPM (Other People's Money), IT strategic alliances also have a business acronym you should deploy. The strategic key to alliance success is using the concept of **O**ther **C**ompany's **K**nowledge **A**nd **D**istribution (OCKAD).

When partnering with other firms, their value to you increases because of your exposure to their knowledge and their product and service distribution. Usage of both of these areas can help you by "piggybacking" your partner's knowledge of successes and failures and expanding your outlets for revenue capture. When partnering with potential alliances, seek out companies whose products or services have a symbiotic attachment with your offerings or whose target market is the same.

Whether partnering with another IT firm or setting up another product or service distribution model, there are both direct and indirect channel options for you to consider. Most firms manage direct sales themselves and use indirect channels to expand into other markets.

Direct channel sales characteristics include:

- Faster return on investment

- Larger gross margin capture

- Replicable and scalable sales process

- Foundation for indirect sales (channel)

- One-to-one leverage

- Primary brand marketing

- Shorter sales cycles

- More accurate sales forecasting

Indirect sales channel distribution characteristics include:

- Longer sales cycles

- Inaccurate sales forecasts

- Decreased margins

- One-to-many leverage

- Secondary brand marketing

- Success is predicated on your direct-sales model success being duplicated

- 80/20 rule of revenue capture where 80% of your channel revenue will come from 20% of your partners

Yet, for all of its limitations, setting up multiple distribution and channel partner programs is still an important business growth concept to be implemented for IT companies.

Note: As electronic demonstration tool usage like webinars increase, and the cost of software and technology decreases, channel partner programs may become an antiquated operating model in the future.

5 Steps to Increase Strategic Partnership Success

1. Partner with companies who have a larger network or partner alliance group than you. Remember, distribution size is a business asset. Take advantage of your partner's circumference of influence. Every company has a sphere of influence made up of a diverse group of customers, prospects, suppliers, and alliances. With this group, there are many opportunities for revenue growth. Each new partner you work with has a circumference of influence circle around them that can be accessed. The most successful strategic-alliance-driven companies we have worked with focus as much on their partner's partners as with the originating partner.

2. Strategic partnerships are about revenue not press releases. Focus on setting up specific revenue goals for each relationship that you establish as a pre-condition for partnership success.

3. Set up a partnership-pursuit sales team that is dedicated to making your strategic alliances more effective. By assigning specific sales team members to this task you increase your alliance success and keep your firm focused.

4. Partnership agreements must be between your senior management and theirs. Never strike a strategic alliance with a business development manager only. Seek corporate commitment from a vice president and above. Even in large companies, go above the local business development manager and get executive commitment and confirmation in writing on the terms and obligations between each partner before moving forward.

5. Dedicate at least one full-time person to strategic partnership development and relationships to make sure it is not a part-time vocation for your firm. Strategic alliances, when done correctly, can help grow any company; when done poorly, it is a waste of time, money, and operational resources.

5 Ways to Use Strategic Partnerships as a Business Tool

1. Participate in tradeshows with your strategic partners; share a tradeshow booth and split each other's prospect lists and booth costs.

2. Work with your partners to create new IT products or service offerings and share the development and marketing costs.

3. Share prospect leads with your partners to increase geometrically the number of leads you and your partners sell to.

4. Co-develop strategic marketing programs and marketing research; send direct mail to each other's prospects databases.

5. Create buying groups with other alliance companies to lower your acquisition costs for common overhead items, including sales, operations, advertising, software, and services rendered by suppliers.

Strategic alliances and partnerships are important tools for any growth-directed CEO. There is no reason to use only your costs and distribution channels when you can leverage others to help.

CEO SUCCESS ACTION STEPS

✓ Decide to increase strategic alliances and partnerships during the next 12 months.

✓ Make a list of industries or companies do you want to establish partnerships with.

✓ Proactively hunt for new partners.

Chapter 15

Hire Management Team Members Based On Your Company's Life-Cycle Model—Not Their Résumé Or How Much They Act Like You

Growing a company requires a management team with depth and one that allows you to replicate and scale your business using a measurable methodology without you being there. Your staff should not be an extension of your ego; or what you want your company to look like to family, friends, customers, or the press; or a mirror image of yourself. Instead, your management team should be a reflection of your weaknesses as a CEO. Employees who lack a depth in their skill sets are merely window dressing and always fail.

Have you ever interviewed a candidate who was extremely professional, polished, and well-spoken and came across as winner? Did you think "Wow, that is the type of team member I want!"? Have you interviewed candidates who seemed to be mini-versions of you? Did you like them? Of course you did—they were carbon copies of you! But that's not the type of management team member you should be looking for. You need to be looking at candidates who enhance your corporate growth needs and fill the gaps in management requirements so your firm can progress to the next level.

Your team needs to be able to backfill your lack of business skill sets as a CEO so that you can maximize your business's success. Often business owners and principals project their needs onto the candidate based on what business functions need to be filled or on the candidate's résumé and what companies he or she previously worked for.

Additionally, it is a rare CEO or business owner who knows enough of the skill sets needed to correctly interview management team members for different department positions.

Are you an engineering, technical, or sales CEO? Have you spent your entire career focused on one company core competence? Do you know what the detailed business requirements are for each department in your company and the specific questions you need to ask a senior accounting person, an operations executive, a major account sales team member, or a marketing manager when you interview them so you can

145

objectively evaluate their ability to help you grow your company?

Probably not—unless you have worked as an accountant, senior salesperson, operations manager, or marketing manager.

What happens in most management team interviews is that the candidate's résumé is reviewed and if it looks solid and the individual sounds more knowledgeable than the CEO in this specific area, and looks better than the other candidates that are being interviewed, they get hired.

Often management teams hire the best candidate available at the time of the open job requisition—<u>not necessarily</u> the best candidate.

Every management person you hire either increases or decreases your business assets based on their ability to efficiently manage their department and position.

If you hire the wrong manager, you can have a department manager sitting in an executive briefing giving incorrect advice to the CEO, who assumes that the managers' business recommendations are correct because the CEO doesn't know any better. Then the CEO implements action steps based on these recommendations and it becomes the blind leading the blind.

Why does this happen? As mentioned before, often candidates are promoted into positions above their level of competence. For example, if a salesperson who is hitting his assigned sales quota starts to complain about career opportunities and the executive team does not want the salesperson to quit because they are afraid of losing their revenue, the salesperson is promoted into sales management. Or, if a marketing staff person has been in your company for five years and she is a loyal employee, she gets promoted to director of marketing. Not because she has a huge knowledge of lead-generation strategies but because she is loyal.

When these people look for jobs at other companies, they include the "management experience" on their résumés and tell potential employers they are experienced managers in their area of specialty. If the next interviewing CEO doesn't know how to evaluate these job skills correctly, then the candidates get hired and the cycle of promotion above their level competency continues and is propitiated forward.

When CEOs incorrectly hire management team members, it decreases their business valuation to prospective buyers because it minimizes the business transfer capabilities due to weak operational infrastructure team skills. Who wants to buy a business where the CEO is the only team member who knows his job?

So, when hiring executive management team members, focus not just on the résumé but also on the specific skill sets needed for them to be successful as department managers and your company's current expansion life cycle needs.

4 Types Of Managers Most Companies Hire

- **Franchise Employees** – These are star team members who know how to manage and are extremely knowledgeable about their position and department. They are self-educated about their department, risk-takers, and students of excellence.

- **Players** – Upcoming franchise players who work hard and are dedicated but don't know all of the best practices, although they are working on it.

- **Homesteaders** – They are average management team members who can do basic supervision but will never be your department leaders. They never take risks and are not self-educated on their job.

- **Sleepwalkers** – These are managers who float through the business day not knowing what they are doing and never seem to be in command of their department intellectually or professionally.

As a CEO, the skills of your management team should supplant the lack of skill sets you have as a manager. You need experienced department managers who fill the gaps of the management knowledge you don't have. In fact, even if you have multidiscipline knowledge of your business, your knowledge is still limited to the concentric circle of experiences you have. By hiring additional management team members, whose experiences are broader than yours, you will diametrically increase your success potential by leveraging their experiences with yours.

When selecting your management team, an often overlooked factor is realizing where your business is in its life cycle to determine what type of management support you need. All companies move through a business life cycle and each phase requires a different management methodology and team member skill set. One reason many new senior managers fail is that their skill sets and job experience do not match the company's current life cycle position.

Business life cycles consist of four separate stages: innovative, growth, mature, and decline. Each stage has a unique skill set requirement for team members and new hires should be selected based on their core competence relevant to the stage of your company's growth is in.

Selecting a candidate who may have the department skill sets needed for your firm but who has the wrong business life cycle stage experience for your company will reduce his or her effectiveness on the job.

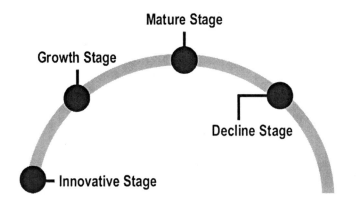

INNOVATIVE BUSINESS LIFE CYCLE STAGE

- Business operating costs are usually high

- Competitors are minimal

- Revenue growth is slow

- Prospect demand must be created

This stage includes IT businesses that are three years old or younger or firms that sell new industry products or services and need to spend a disproportionate amount of their funding on marketing, advertising, and buyer education to encourage prospects to buy.

During the innovative stage, your offering's business value is being communicated, discussed, and evaluated by your buyers while your offering's distribution is being developed and implemented. Based on what you sell, pricing during this stage will offer you the highest gross margin potential, which has to be managed because of high marketing and development costs.

Types of management to hire: Franchise employees and Players

GROWTH BUSINESS LIFE CYCLE STAGE

- Corporate profits begin to increase

- Sales volume increases aggressively

- Operational costs drop

- Market competitors increase

During this stage, business revenue increases and business costs decrease because your targeted market starts to understand your business value and distribution channels are being increased.

Depending on your industry and what technology and professional services you sell, the timeline for a growth business life cycle can be from three to ten years. As you become successful during this stage, competitors start entering the market. Simultaneously, your gross margin decreases while your volume picks up.

Types of management to hire: Franchise employees and Players

MATURE BUSINESS LIFE CYCLE STAGE

- Market demand for what you sell flattens

- Prices are reduced due to increased competition

- Corporate profits decrease

- More competitors enter the market

- Operation costs drop because of higher volumes and decreased industry knowledge

During this stage, buyer demand remains level because aggressive competitors have entered the market, which forces your product or service pricing to flatten and become a commodity. Often you are forced into price wars, discounting, and value-positioning beliefs that you are like your competition.

Types of management to hire: Players and Homesteaders

DECLINE BUSINESS LIFE CYCLE STAGE

- Corporate profits are reduced as production drops

- Prospect demand shrinks aggressively

- Revenues drop dramatically

During this stage, revenues and buyer demand are decreasing, value is not discernible amongst competitors, marketing and sales costs are increasing, and some competitors are leaving the market.

Types of management to hire: Franchise employees and Players

When hiring a corporate manager, you need to find executives whose management capabilities and business experience parallel your company's current or next stage business life cycle . . . not just their department knowledge.

Why?

Although department knowledge is important for successful leadership, it is also critical to have the ability to use that knowledge operating under different business models and national economic markets. Hiring management team members because their résumés reflect deep department knowledge without knowing what business life cycle they have been successful in is a process for failure.

An additional variable that must be considered when evaluating a management candidate is the annual revenue of their current or past employer. Interviewing a vice president of sales or a chief financial officer (CFO) for a new position from a $75 million per year competitor, when you are a $7 million a year company is a serious mistake. The cultural and organizational environment is so different between the two companies that transposing an executive from a much larger company to your company is too big of an operating jump for the candidate to statistically be an asset to your team.

Are these candidates ever successful? Of course, but more often than not, the impact of a bad hire for your business is way beyond the fully loaded expense of carrying a non-producing executive—it is the bad decisions they supply.

When doing due diligence of potential management candidates for your executive team, focus on the life cycle position of the company(ies) they have worked for as well as the annual revenues of the companies. Never hire a manager from a company that is more than **five times** your annual revenues unless they can prove they have moved from varying sized companies during their career and been successful.

CEO SUCCESS ACTION STEPS

✓ Hire team members based on your company's life cycle and the executive's skill sets.

✓ Decide what business life cycle your firm is currently in.

✓ Determine your executive team's current management type

Finance Manager:_____

Sales Manager:_____

Marketing Manager:_____

Operations/Engineering Manager:_____

Other:_____

Chapter 16

Manage by a Developed Strategy— Not Emotion!

We expect all our businesses to have a positive impact on our top and bottom lines. Profitability is very important to us or we wouldn't be in this business.
—Jeff Bezos, CEO/Founder, Amazon.com

To be successful in today's economy, CEOs must move from an entrepreneurial management process to a professional management process.

Are there entrepreneurial run IT companies that are successful?

Yes.

Can entrepreneurial management processes make a company successful? Yes, but it limits long-term growth because it is not a scalable or replicable business model that is sustainable because the CEO/founder is usually the key business driver—who cannot be replaced.

In privately held companies where the founder is in the position of Vice President of Sales or the key senior technologist thought leader, the company's business valuation is often reduced to outside investors. Why? Because if the founder becomes sick or is killed in a car accident, the company's growth model comes to a halt. Watch the Wall Street stock movements of public companies like Apple and Oracle as they fluctuate based on the health news of their respective executive management.

Another key business driver that distinguishes entrepreneurial management business processes from professional management processes is the use of a detailed strategy, financial statements, and business metrics to monitor company performance, drive staff success, and increase revenue. Simply being a successful high tech CEO who can close deals for the sales team with your eyes closed or a program coder extraordinaire who can write applications better than anyone is not enough.

In today's market, IT CEOs must lead not only by tactical action steps, but also with a developed and communicated strategy and with the knowledge of their firm's income, expenses, and return on investments that allows their business to operate independently of them. With the correct use of financial statements, developed strategy, and business metrics, you can manage your business cycle to success, year after year—even if you are not always there.

> *The trouble with the business cycle is that*
> *there just aren't enough people pedaling.*
> *—Sharyn Katalinich*

To be a professional high tech CEO you must make decisions based on facts and data rather than on personal experience or assumptions. When making executive decisions, there are five IT business success asset areas you must manage metrically. They are:

1. Human Capital Assets

2. Financial Assets

3. Sales and Marketing Assets

4. Operations/Delivery Assets

5. Customer Assets

These areas each need to have established metrics to manage them proactively instead of reactively. They should be aligned together as tools to drive revenue and work in parallel in an integrated approach. These assets are not independent department silos but are all key business assets that are interrelated and must be managed as such.

Focus on these five business assets and you increase your firm's ability to grow and prosper.

1.   Human Capital Assets

Even in a poor economic market, your employees are a business asset that you must manage and invest in. Finding good team members is not easy. Measuring employee performance is also not easy. So, hire slow and terminate fast, because employees either make you money—or cost you money.

The *minimum top metrics* you want to manage monthly for human capital assets are:

- Annual revenue per employee

- Annual profit before taxes per employee per year

- Percentage of employee turnover by department per year

- Annual cost of training per employee per year

2.   Financial Assets Metrics

Most high tech CEOs have monthly P and Ls and depending on their interests, their senior financial executives' input, and the size of their company, some regular detail that outlines in general how their IT company is doing on a regular basis.

Here are the minimum P and L details you need to monitor monthly:

- Cash Flow—over/under analysis calculated by comparing your A/P against your A/R over 12 weeks to calculate the cash flow in weeks and where there is a gap

- Percentage of rent to sales

- Total percentage of payroll to sales

- Gross margin for each IT product and service you sell

- Gross revenue for each IT product and service you sell

- P and L by department with line item detail

3.   Sales and Marketing Assets

Like other business assets, sales and marketing must be managed monthly through metrics. Here are the minimum metrics you should track:

- Amount of new customer sales as a percentage of total revenue—your goal should be 50% of total revenue from new business from new customers

- Percentage of existing customer sales as a total of revenue

- Percentage of sales forecast accuracy month to month—75% accuracy is the minimum goal

- Size (both dollar and percent) of sales pipeline as compared to sales forecast

- Cost per marketing lead

- Number of leads needed to make one sale

- Percent of closing from proposals submitted

4. Operations/Delivery Assets

The minimum operations department metrics you should track monthly include:

- Cost per delivery, installation, or training hour

- Cost of inbound support per hour

- Bench utilization rate of billable staff

- Number of support calls made per day

- Number of support calls closed per day

- Number of support calls not closed and carried into the next day

5. Customer Assets

- Lifetime dollar value of each customer over the last three to five years and the projected dollar value over the next five years

- Percentage of customer leakage (loss) per year

- Five-year revenue replacement model of timed sales programs consisting of new IT products and services that are named and priced to sell to your existing clients over 5 years

Additionally, to complement metric management direction, your accounting system should also be an IT business success tool. Set up all of your departments' financial statements with line-item detail that shows technology, software, and service income and expenses, including:

- This year's actual revenue against budgeted revenue

- This year's actual revenue against last year's actual revenue

- This year's revenue percentage of budget against last year's revenue percentage of budget

- This year's percentage of total budget for revenue and expenses as compared to last year's percentage of revenue and expenses

- Set up separate IT product and service profitability analysis for *each business vertical industry* you sell into. This will allow you to determine gross profit and average discount for each industry you sell and for each IT offering you market.

Once you have this data from all departments, use it to increase your company's success.

- **Review** your financial statements carefully. **Assess** what needs to be adjusted. **Take action** steps to correct what needs to be changed. Use the **RATA** formula to manage your P&Ls: Review your P&Ls, Assess the variables of your P&Ls that need to be adjusted, and Take Action for all departments based on your observations.

- Focus on expense management first—this is an item you can immediately adjust

- Focus on revenue gaps to determine areas in your forecast that need adjustment

- Isolate the details of the variance gaps and set up an action list

- Set up all departments with separate P&Ls by geographic zones (or offices) for each product and service you sell and then as a consolidated P&L as a whole

- Set up all P&Ls before corporate, general, and administrative overhead (G & A)

- All P&Ls should include budget, revenue, and expenses from the previous year and the current year. Once a month, hold a management meeting to discuss the P&Ls in detail

- Review your chart of accounts coding to make sure it is accurate

- Manage gross margin for each IT product you sell

- Manage gross margin for each IT service you sell

- If you have a field service department, manage corporate inventory by person; develop asset tags for inventory

- Pre-package training costs for each product and service you sell (sell training; don't just take orders)

- Manage implementation costs for each product and service you sell through an individualized customer sales P&L

- Never sell any new IT product or service unless operations and engineering pre-plan its absorption into your company—plan first; sell second

- Manage operations/engineering as a profit center (separate from sales) and create outbound-revenue-capture programs independent from the sales department that allows Operations to prosper independently from the sale effort. If this requires you to have your own sales and marketing efforts separate from the sales department, then so be it.

CEO SUCCESS ACTION STEPS

✓ Design P&L statements with line-item detail.

✓ Hold monthly meetings with department heads to manage all departments by P&L.

✓ Discuss the data you want the P&L statements to provide with your financial management team.

✓ Determine when you want to schedule monthly meetings (i.e., the first Monday of the month, the last business day of the month, etc.).

Chapter 17

Use a Revenue Capture Scorecard to Monitor Your Company's Performance

It's Business Results—Not the Products Or Services You Sell—That Count

A s mentioned earlier, prior to starting my own companies, I was Vice President of Worldwide Strategic Development for Renaissance Worldwide, a public company headquartered in Boston. Renaissance was originally called The Registry, Inc., which purchased a consulting firm called Renaissance Solutions Inc., whose principals, Robert Kaplan and David Norton, wrote a management success book titled BALANCED SCORECARD. The Balanced Scorecard management methodology is a dominant strategy used worldwide by global 1000 companies. To better reflect its corporate strategic management direction, The Registry changed its name to Renaissance Worldwide and centered the business model on the balanced scorecard approach. So, as the senior corporate strategy executive, I worked directly for the CEO and the board of directors and was cognizant of this business process.

After observing the balanced scorecard's original process, I identified a strategic gap in its usage. The balanced scorecard is a strong management tool for large established multi-national companies such as Ford, IBM, American Express, and others where their business success is well established. But what about smaller growth-directed companies?

As a result, I created another management tool called the Revenue Capture Scorecard® which is different. It focuses on revenue-capture. It aligns sales, marketing, strategy, and financial management areas into a controlled outbound-revenue-capture process. The purpose of using a Revenue Capture Scorecard is to develop specific qualitative objectives that are measured monthly for each of these four areas (sales, marketing, strategy, and financial management) to help your company create a visual tool of performance to grow your business—not just manage it. These four areas are linked together for true company revenue capture success. The alignment and linkage of these areas is a key underlining foundation of making a scorecard management tool work correctly (i.e., sales cannot go up if marketing does not generate qualified leads). If you are selling a blue shoe to a red shoe market, your strategy is not aligned correctly with buyer demand, which will negatively affect your revenue growth potential.

When used correctly, Revenue Capture Scorecards help you and your team members visually monitor their individual performances and how those performances affect the alignment with each department.

How to Set Up a Revenue Capture Scorecard

Use Microsoft Excel and list each of the four areas in its own column. Next, list objectives for each area by week for the period of a month. Link each perspective to all others to coordinate consistent segment progress.

Use color coded Excel cells to visually conform the status of the action step goal:

1. **Red** = Missed Objectives

2. **Green** = Accomplished Objectives

3. **Yellow** = Warning! About To Miss Objectives

4. **Green** = Tasks are completed

5. **Red** = Tasks are not completed

REVENUE CAPTURE SCORECARD EXAMPLE:

Sales Scorecard				
Date	1-Jul	8-Jul	15-Jul	22-Jul
Timetable	Week 1	Week 2	Week 3	Week 4
Sales Dept.				
Cold Calls				
Presentations				
Closed Deals				
Hire New Reps				
Strategy Dept.				
Open new Boston office				
Launch a new IT service in LA				
Raise software pricing				
Finance Dept.				
Margin goals for service met				
Sales costs on target				
A/R on maintenance agreements under 45 days				
Marketing Dept.				
Sent out direct mail				
Completed draft of brochure copy				
Sent out press release				

Implement these scorecards to be measured monthly and focus on the red cells in the spreadsheet, where you or your team members have missed the objectives. Concentrate on completing these objectives monthly. Break down IT revenue growth into digestible steps that can be managed. Simultaneously, it gives you and your team visual management tools that all can understand. When used correctly, scorecards become a proactive task management tool for you and your team to work in tandem on.

Managing your business professionally requires a premeditated process where your ego and personal needs are subordinate to corporate growth and business goals that use facts, metrics, and financial statements as decision-making criteria.

As an entrepreneur, you have a choice.

CEO SUCCESS ACTION STEPS

- ✓ Set up a Revenue Capture Scorecard for your firm.

- ✓ Use the scorecard monthly as a business success management tool.

- ✓ Focus on red objectives which are not being met.

Chapter 18

Use Business Valuations as a Growth Tool

When we work with merger and acquisition clients, many of them are surprised and often depressed when their business valuation for sale is calculated the first time. Business value is never what entrepreneurs think it should be. Unlike public companies whose stock price and book value are measured every day, private companies normally do not know what their business value is until it is too late.

If you are a privately held IT company, you and/or your family have blood, sweat, and tears built into the business, accumulated through the personal and financial sacrifices you have endured to get the company to its current position. But, your financial contributions and lack of available family time are not relevant to a factual value estimation of your business success and worth to another buyer or investor.

One way to accurately calculate your business value year after year and to create manageable benchmarks of how successful you truly are is by getting an annual independent business valuation of what your business is worth. Most IT companies do not plan their business sale since selling a business is often an unplanned process driven by the CEO's health, a family medical or personal emergency, financial needs, or just founder boredom. Hence a business valuation is a last-minute calculation.

By having an independent discounted-cash-flow (DCF) valuation of your business by a third party, you can establish corporate growth goals that can be tracked and measured. Even if you are not looking to sell your business in the near term, business valuations identify how your business is doing objectively because your valuation calculation is not emotionally attached or financially connected with your personal needs. As the valuation price moves up and down, it will confirm or adjust your perception on how well your business is doing and help you make strategic and tactical decisions based on what you think your business should be worth.

What does a business valuation cost? Depending on where you are located, what kind of IT business you operate, and what your annual revenues are, a business valuation will cost between $3,000 and $50,000 or more—but it is well worth the investment. The cost should be built into your annual budget and implemented as a success scorecard key performance indicator. Don't be cheap and say you don't need it until you sell the business. That's the kind of attitude amateur business people make.

To be successful, you need defined quantitative metrics; an annual business valuation is one of those metrics.

CEOs Can Use Business Valuations to Increase Their Company Success

Having an annual valuation performed on your business helps management teams strategically identify success gaps in their marketing, operations, finance, strategy, and sales programs. When done correctly, valuations pinpoint business cash-flow issues, strategy needs, and operations' issues and produce an independent third-party view of your business value from a potential buyer's point of view that is not financially or emotionally attached to the seller's needs.

There are many methodologies used to calculate a company's business valuation, including:

- **Book Value:** The book value of a business is based on the accounting records and is determined simply by subtracting the company's liabilities from its assets.

- **Discounted Cash Flow:** This valuation method uses the projected future unencumbered cash flow of the company (meeting all liabilities) discounted by the firm's weighted average cost of capital (the average cost of all the capital used in the business, including debt and equity), plus a risk factor beta that is calculated and measured.

- **Market Value (Public Companies):** The market value is calculated by multiplying the quoted share price of the company by the number of issued shares.

- **Asset Accumulation:** The asset approach is based on the value of the business if you liquidated or sold off the property, plant, and equipment (PP&E) assets of the company and paid off all of the company's liabilities. The net proceeds would accrue to the equity of the company.

- **Multiple Valuation Methods (sales, EBITA, etc.):** Business value is calculated based on a multiplier of the company's annual sales and/or its earnings and compared to other similar business sales within its industry (and sometimes its geography) to get a buyer comparable. This model often looks at intellectual property valuation based on a roll-up added value as well.

- **Price Earnings Multiple Valuation:** The price-earnings ratio (P/E) is simply the price of a company's share of common stock in the public market place divided by its earnings per share.

When IT companies seek to be sold, often a central driver in calculating their potential sales price is market comparables. However, using market comparables or a hybrid calculation year over year is not a consistent tool for determining a sales price or valuation that can be used as a management benchmark tool because competitive valuations are always fluctuating based on the buyer demand.

Of the six methods mentioned above, method number two—*Discounted Cash Flow*—is the best CEO management growth guidance tool to help you understand your current success level by analyzing the true available cash your business throws off so a qualified buyer can calculate your business's true worth and their return on investment if they buy. Even if you have no short-term exit strategy planned, knowing what your business is worth can help drive your business decisions better. If the valuation is low compared to what you think it should be, it helps you identify the growth goals you need to focus on. Use business valuations as a strategic business driver and annual yardstick to make better decisions.

To measure your business success, get a business valuation every year.

CEO SUCCESS ACTION STEPS

✓ Get a business valuation to determine what your company's benchmarks are.

✓ Determine what is your goal is for next year's business valuation.

✓ Use your annual IT business valuation as a measurement tool of where you are and where you want to be.

Chapter 19

Invest in Your Company

It's not a private bank . . . it's your business!

Every CEO who starts, buys, or inherits (and even some who are hired in) a company believes that the company is *their* company. Equity-wise, it may be, but if you have employees it is their company, too. Why? Because employees are part of your business's assets and you need to invest in your assets to increase your equity.

Consider your answers to the following questions:

- As CEO, are you paying yourself too much?

- Is your spouse on the payroll and not working in the business?

- Are your kids driving company cars?

- Are your vacations written off as client meetings?

Business Revenue First; Corporate, General, and Administrative Costs Second

Oftentimes at the Value Forward Group, we recast our clients' private company financial statements to give them a business metric comparison of their financials against their competitors from our proprietary financial management database. We often see profit and loss statements that are riddled with owner perks, family member's payroll checks, extravagant vacations, expensive cars, and lavish gifts to the principals.

Is it important for business owners—who take all of the financial and emotional risks of entrepreneurship—to maximize their return on investment to themselves? Of course, but not if it jeopardizes the foundational elements of your business success and what afforded you the compensation and benefits you are pulling out. Additionally, as soon as your company starts hiring and growing staff members, you obligate (morally and professionally) yourself to supporting and compensating your team fairly, based on your mutual goals of working together to grow the business and your need to enrich owner's equity.

I once listened to a client (a CEO of a $20 million IT project management company) debate with his wife (and co-business owner) why they should reduce their personal business income from $3 million per year to $2 million a year so they could use the additional $1 million of cash flow to add management team members. Their conversation went on for over an hour as they discussed how they would struggle living on *only* $2 million a year . . . but they would be able to reduce their weekly hours from eighty to sixty if they made the investment and built an infrastructure that would allow them to sell the business in the future.

Ultimately logic won over emotion and my client reduced their income. They went on to build a replicable and scalable business, adding a management infrastructure that continues to grow top line revenue today.

When business principals withdraw disproportionate amounts of company cash to their benefit and not the business' benefit, they reduce their business valuation resell opportunities, minimize their credit line and bank funding potential, devalue their corporate assets (their employees), and destabilize corporate breakevens.

Having started multiple businesses myself, I appreciate personal enrichment—but the key word here is *business* not *bank*. Don't just make withdrawals. You also have to make deposits.

In any growth business, the biggest intellectual property (asset) you have is your staff. In good economies or bad, it is always difficult to find qualified, hard-working employees. So, to maximize your company's growth potential, you have to invest in this asset (your staff) over and over again to increase its return on investment.

Recommended Compensation for Growth- and Success-Directed CEOs

The hardest decision for any company founder who is moving from start-up to growth mode is when to add employees and what to pay him or herself. Below are some compensation guidelines for CEOs of growth-directed firms:

- If you are the sole employee of a privately held IT company, have no investors, work at least seventy hours a week, and the cash flow allows it, pay yourself at least $100,000 per year plus benefits, before you hire someone. (Some business coaches disagree and suggest that you should not pay yourself this type of salary even if you can afford to until after you hire your first employee . . . but this wrong.) As an entrepreneur, you must reward yourself for your hard work and commitment.

- Once you pay yourself at least $100,000 a year, think about hiring your first employee.

- Once you have employees, never pay yourself more than 10% of gross revenues until you have built a replicable and scalable business that can replace you and until you invest at least 5% of your gross revenue back into the company for new IT product, service development, and employee training.

- Pay all of your good employees (based on their job description success) 5% to 10% above market to lock them into a long-term commitment based on your display of appreciation.

CEO SUCCESS ACTION STEPS

✓ Don't withdraw company funds disproportionate to your company's short-term and long-term goals. Manage your company's cash so that you can invest in your team's learning skills, your business infrastructure development, and other assets.

✓ Invest at least 5% of gross revenues in staff training and new product and services development.

✓ Research what market compensation is for each of your employees' positions.

✓ Determine if you paying your best employees at least 10% above market.

Chapter 20

Stop Being a King in the Kingdom and Start Managing Employees as Team Contributors and Your Business as a Business

Okay, you or your parents started a business and things are going well. I get it—but stop acting like the king in the kingdom. Just because you are the CEO does not mean you know everything. Just because the compensation you pay yourself is far greater than your peer group, friends, or family does not mean you know what you are doing. As previously discussed, your business could be successful in spite of your contribution.

> *Equity ownership or personal compensation payment is not a measurement of business knowledge.*

To determine if you act like the king of a kingdom, take the following test.

1. Do you ever ask for advice and actually use it?

   ☐ Yes   ☐ No

2. Do you hire third-party advisors or consultants on a regular basis and use their advice?

   ☐ Yes   ☐ No

3. Do you yell at employees and tell them, "It's my company, do it my way"?

   ☐ Yes   ☐ No

4. Do you take credit for employees' ideas when they have success?

   ☐ Yes   ☐ No

5. Is the majority of management related to you by blood or marriage?

   ☐ Yes   ☐ No

6. Do you take a disproportionate amount of compensation for yourself irrelevant to the company's business needs?

   ☐ Yes   ☐ No

7. Do you have detailed written job descriptions and metrics for employees to be measured by?

    ☐ Yes   ☐ No

8. Do you yell at or threaten employees often to get them to perform their assigned job tasks?

    ☐ Yes   ☐ No

9. Have you ever dated, seduced, or flirted with an employee?

    ☐ Yes   ☐ No

10. When your decisions go wrong, do you blame employees?

    ☐ Yes   ☐ No

ANSWERS

1. Yes	6. No
2. Yes	7. Yes
3. No	8. No
4. No	9. No
5. No	10. No

SCORING

Each correct answer is worth 10%.

80% and Above

You are **not** a king in the kingdom and you manage your business professionally.

50% to 70%

You move between being a professional manager and a king in the kingdom depending on the issue of the day. You need to be cautious in your comments and actions, because your team members may not see you as you see yourself.

Below 50%

You are a king in the kingdom . . . and you know it. You probably enjoy your approach to management and have megalomaniac beliefs about yourself. Your business success and failure will always be tied to your personality and is not replicable or scalable, thereby reducing your business assets and/or limiting your exit strategy.

Build a Business—Not a Job

Increase your business success by building your business to sell (even if you are not going to sell). Do you have an exit strategy for you, your family, and management team?

Exit-Strategy Checklist

1. Are your financial statements filled with personal expenses?

    ☐ Yes ☐ No

2. Are your financial statements set up to show line-item detail of profit and loss by each department before and after corporate, general, and administrative expenses?

    ☐ Yes ☐ No

3. Do you reinvest at least 5% of your company's gross revenues into business asset improvement areas like new product and service development, employee training, and physical assets betterment?

    ☐ Yes ☐ No

4. Do you have a written sales process that lists step by step how to sell a prospect?

    ☐ Yes ☐ No

5. Do you have written job descriptions and compensation plans for all employees?

    ☐ Yes ☐ No

6. Do you have a written prospect demographic profile of your most likely customer?

   ☐ Yes   ☐ No

7. Do you have a management team that can operate your business successfully without you?

   ☐ Yes   ☐ No

8. Is part of your management team's compensation based on their department's profitability?

   ☐ Yes   ☐ No

9. Do you hold weekly executive management team meetings?

   ☐ Yes   ☐ No

10. Can you manage your business off premise by the weekly reports you receive?

    ☐ Yes   ☐ No

11. Does less than 10% of your total company revenue come from one customer?

    ☐ Yes   ☐ No

12. Does at least 50% of your total company revenue come from new business from new prospects?

    ☐ Yes   ☐ No

13. Has your business revenue increased at least 20% per year, year over year, for the last three years?

    ☐ Yes   ☐ No

14. Do you have a written succession plan in place, for your managers and family, in case you pass on?

    ☐ Yes   ☐ No

15. Do you have a written strategic business plan that is updated yearly?

    ☐ Yes   ☐ No

16. Is more than 30% of the management team related to you by marriage or by lineage?

    ☐ Yes   ☐ No

17. Is your total employee turnover more than 20% per year?

    ☐ Yes   ☐ No

18. Do you have "key man executive" insurance on yourself?

    ☐ Yes   ☐ No

19. Are your accounts receivables under 90 days?

    ☐ Yes   ☐ No

20. Have you legally identified and secured the intellectual property (customer base, operations methodology, technology, etc.) of your company?

    ☐ Yes   ☐ No

ANSWERS

1. No	6. Yes	11. Yes	16. No
2. Yes	7. Yes	12. Yes	17. Yes
3. Yes	8. Yes	13. Yes	18. Yes
4. Yes	9. Yes	14. Yes	19. Yes
5. Yes	10. Yes	15. No	20. Yes

SCORING

Each correct answer is worth 5%.

<u>75% and above</u>
You are a professional manager who understands that your employees are part of your company's assets and you have an exit-ready company.

50% to 70%
You are a professional manager depending on where your business agenda takes you and the labors of the day.

Below 50%
Due to your current management style, you are not building a replicable and scalable business with assets (your team) that are transferable and are reducing your IT business's success transfer capabilities.

CEO SUCCESS ACTION STEPS

✓ Decide how you will change your management style to accomplish more.

Chapter 21

Work With Your Board of Directors & Partners

A board of directors is a body of elected or appointed members who jointly oversee the activities of a company or organization.
—From Wikipedia, the free encyclopedia

Oftentimes during our business strategy meetings with executive management teams, the subject of action step approval by other company partners and/or the board of directors is discussed. These influences, although not to be ignored, sometimes hang like a yoke around the CEO and the executive management team's decision process. Like the invisible elephant in the room, pros and cons are weighed based on what the board will say.

As described by Wikipedia, a board of directors consists of appointed members who jointly oversee the activities of a company—your company, your investor's company, or your partner's company.

If the corporate goal is to grow your IT business's top-line revenues and bottom-line profitability, then the key to successful strategy is action—not hesitation and extended deliberation. Yes, you have to evaluate strategic decisions, to prevent missteps and budget fiascos, but ultimately most boards want success too. Their knowledge or lack of knowledge may be apparent in how they perceive the CEO should accomplish this mutual goal but the outcome should be the same.

To be a successful, professional IT CEO, you need to learn how to work with your board of directors based on their success goals and yours.

7 GUIDELINES ON HOW TO SUCCESSFULLY WORK WITH YOUR BOARD OF DIRECTORS

1. **Don't communicate too much detail to the board—but communicate often.**

   Board of directors consume information, but giving them too much detail can make them move from an advisor at a distance to a granular in your face—an I-know-everything-let-me-tell-you-how-to-do-it committee. Keep the board informed between meetings, supply general information on key business events and financial positioning, but leave details out until pressed by members or needed to sway a decision.

2. **You and the executive team must work with the Board in tandem.**

   Your board of directors is not the enemy. You and your executive team must learn to operate under the board's umbrella. When the CEO feels antagonistic to the board, it trickles down to the rest of the executive management team and becomes the del facto attitude that permeates how everyone responds to a board request.

3. **Listen to the board members—but do what you need to do to be successful.**

   The skill sets of a board of directors fluctuates based on their corporate governance and the chairman's influence. Some board members give direct, specific suggestions on corporate strategy success to executive teams that may or may not be valid. But CEOs need to listen to these suggestions because it is politically correct to do so—and to gleam the business experiences and advice good board members can bring to a high tech company.

   But, it's your job and ultimately you are going to be held accountable. Trying to defend a strategic position or executive decision based on what a board member suggested is a losing battle.

4. **Tell the truth, good or bad.**

Beyond legalities and corporate governance, the board hates surprises. When you have good news, tell them. When you have bad news, tell them. If you are truly working with the board in tandem you must share the knowledge you have about your company's success or lack of success as it happens, not after the fact.

5. **Know your business better than anyone. It is hard for board members to disagree with documented facts, metrics, and data.**

It's late in the day and a board member calls you to check in on a rumor he or she heard about a business decision that you made. Do you know the facts and the details on why you made that decision? When CEOs don't have command knowledge about their business or can't get factual information fast, it reduces board members' perception of your leadership skills. They think the CEO is not in control. When dealing with board members, use data as decision-validation tools to help communicate your leadership strength and position. More facts equal fewer questions from the board.

6. **Build a personal relationship with at least two board members.**

   When working with boards, always develop a personal relationship with at least two strategic board members who can help you navigate through the process. Having inside board coaches (who also represent two votes) that can mentor you will increase your success with the board, both in your presentation approach and their understanding of your decision-making process. Like selling a key account, inside board member coaches can lead you through the mine field to the desired outcome.

7. **Be decisive. Take actions steps. Manage your business, so the board does not have to.**

   Being action oriented is a great IT CEO skill set. Boards want action. In today's economic market space, making tough decisions is what boards want. You are the CEO. Prove it to the board that you are the right executive by managing your business as needed and with objective decisions.

CLIENT CASE STUDY

I was working with a West Coast VC-funded, Silicon Valley IT firm, whose offering, a vertical industry B2B client server application, had gone into commodity mode and was currently breaking even.

Five years ago, their app sold for $350,000 with 22% annual maintenance and support fees. But the market had gone into a SaaS model (Software As A Service), where their competitors were now charging $3,000 to $4,000 a month.

For three years, the firm had kept its programming team deep in domestic code development trying to move the client server application to a SaaS model. But, after spending $7 million, they were still two years away from releasing their Internet app and only had $4 million left of their investor's money.

Simultaneously, their maintenance revenue was dropping $1 million a year while existing customers, frustrated with the lack of upgrade offerings, migrated to their SaaS competitors.

After huddling with the executive team through an intensive strategy success assessment, I concluded that their current roadmap would ultimately be their demise. During our analysis, we discovered they had also created a new SaaS application for another client. Its market potential, at least based on preliminary market gap research, was actually greater than their current model. So, after meeting with the CEO and the management team, we suggested that the company go into maintenance mode for one year, cut the sales, marketing, admin, and operations team members by 50% and reduce all development on their current offering to just needed bug fixes. We then suggested that they take their new unique, one-of-a-kind app and do a detailed market gap analysis to determine if market demand was greater than supply. If, after the gap was researched and there was a sustainable SaaS market that had a gap they could succeed in, we suggested they should develop the complete new application offering offshore in a 7/24 (with a detailed spec) programming environment. Once it was ready, I suggested that they hire back the sales and market staff and create a new outbound-revenue capture program and hunt for new business.

When presented to the client, they agreed that their current market direction was doomed to failure, that their investors would not fund them another round, and that they would ultimately run out cash.

They also agreed that investigating the new SaaS app market gap potential was imperative to their company's future. But, the CEO wavered on the recommendations I gave him to reduce his burn rate by freezing his current IT development and releasing half of his staff. His concern was that the board of directors would not like this and would see it as a sign of his poor management and would question his leadership skills to date.

I told the CEO, that the board would take these action steps as a positive sign of his leadership skills because the IT industry is a dynamic, ever-changing market space and he was making the right decisions needed to make the company successful again.

He ultimately rejected my recommendations to cut development and sales and marketing staff overhead. He did implement the market gap analysis for the new application and discovered a growth opportunity where demand was greater than supply. Ultimately, he ran out of cash while he was developing the new application while also maintaining the old application and they had to shut their doors.

CEO Success Action Steps

✓ Develop a structured plan to improve your communication with your investors and board of directors.

✓ Work with your board of directors using information as a business tool.

Chapter 22

Make Decisive and Speedy Executive Decisions

Fail Fast – Forward – you can fail, just do it fast and move forward.
—Carol Bartz - Former CEO AutoDesk

All high tech assets must be managed proactively. Being decisive is a key driver that increases your return on investments.

Adaptability and Speed are high tech Business Success Drivers

Do you have a written strategic plan? Is it older than one year? Three years? It is almost impossible to build an accurate, use as a blueprint, three-year strategic plan for a high tech company. Why? Because the technological market and the economy change so much that no one can predict three years out—and even one year just becomes a guess.

CLIENT CASE STUDY

A privately held, 250 million Euros international system integrator (SI) firm headquartered in the United Kingdom and that operated in the Middle East and Africa, was trying to make a decision to either sell or expand its struggling business unit that supported the insurance and banking industries. After doing a success assessment, the Value Forward Group recommended that they keep the unit and reinvest in its assets. But, the executive team could not decide if this operating unit was the right strategic fit and let the 35 million Euros unit flounder without new technology investments or leadership guidance. Over the next two years, this group's revenue and business valuation simultaneously decreased.

As the management team went back and forth on this decision process, the general manager of the business unit went to the executive team and offered to buy the division with private equity investors. But the SI firm still pondered. Ultimately, the division general manager bought the business unit at a price of one-fifth of the original offer and today, as a standalone company, it has grown revenue year over year and is at an 80 million Euros annual run rate.

The high tech market is a speed market.

As a high tech CEO how fast do you move? How adaptable are you and your team?

Who could forecast ten years ago that real estate, airline reservation systems, and bookstores would be dominated by Internet players today?

If you feel that fast change in your firm is a distraction and that that adjustments to your IT product offering or price or market model modifications must be implemented at a controllable pace to minimize employee and company disorientation—you are wrong.

The IT industry is volatile by its very design. It is not waiting for you to decide that you are comfortable with your current pace of management decisions, it is changing while you're still thinking.

In 1975, as Microsoft was completing its rollout of the new, much-delayed GUI application called Windows 95, Bill Gates acknowledged that his company was falling technically behind Internet companies like America Online and Netscape. To respond to this technology change and his company's lagging position he publicly dictated that within two years all current and future Microsoft applications would be Internet operational. With one direct public commitment, Bill Gates took his multibillion dollar company, with tens of thousands of employees, and changed his organizational structure from an aircraft carrier into a speed boat and attacked the market. Through internal development and strategic acquisitions, he changed his employee cultural and financial operations success model and never looked back.

In 1999, as most large enterprise application companies were trying to manage the increased volume of business they were getting from Global 1000 companies seeking to control the perceived Y2K millennium bug problems, Oracle changed its business model and released their Oracle8i application, the first Internet enterprise resource application offering.

Again, there is that adaptability and speed thing.

In 1996, two Stanford University students started to work on an Internet search engine called "Backrub." During the first years of their business timeline, they struggled to find a financial business model where they could make money. On June 1, 1999, a company called GoTo.com released a new toolset application to manage Pay Per Click (PPC) Advertising—a new pay-as-you-go Internet marketing model that became a cash cow for other Internet search engine companies.

By the year 2000, Backrub had changed its name to Google and was funded by VCs and surrounded by hundreds of Internet search engine competitors.

In October 2000, Google identified that a PPC model would be adaptable to their mathematical algorithm search engine, quickly adapted their model, and released a new application called Adwords that used a Pay Per Click advertising approach to generate revenue.

This change was implemented so fast by Google that it diametrically changed their operating business model and corporate culture overnight—and the industry as a whole— creating a new business paradigm . . . of course, the rest is history.

The common variables of these case studies is that these high tech business founders focused on adaptability based on market needs and speed to take their IT firms to the next level. Studying the market and changing as needed was the key. They did not vacillate on can we do it or will my staff adapt or we did not invent it here—they just did it.

So, if you are a $5, $20, $100 million or larger privately held IT company struggling with perceptions that your firm cannot adapt culturally or professionally to needed business changes to take your firm to the next level—stop procrastinating.

Like the Nike slogan says: "Just do it."

If large, bureaucratic, public companies with stockholders and tens of thousands of employees can change, why can't you?

Use speed as an IT business asset and you will grow revenue faster.

The 1% Twelve-Month Program to Greater Growth

Sometimes, being a high tech CEO is boring. Sometimes being a high tech CEO is tedious. You have to manage HR issues, difficult clients, high maintenance salespeople, development shops that are always behind schedule, and a Board of Directors that wants actions not hope.

The fun part of being CEO is when business is booming and your firm can do no wrong.

When working with growth-directed IT clients we often find management teams seeking to raise their bar of success fast by shooting for a huge jump in revenues year over year. They seek revenue growth of 25%, 50% or more per annum.

That is when business becomes fun again.

But, is that possible? Yes and no.

Yes, in a technology market niche that is unexploited, where demand is greater than supply, where your business assets are being maximized, and where your company departments are perfectly aligned with your infrastructure assets—it can happen.

But, mathematically this type of growth is not a sustainable replicable model that can operate in perpetuity. So, the Value Forward Group developed the 1% Twelve-Month Program to Greater Growth that gives technology companies a manageable success process that can be utilized consistently in any economic market environment and for any length of time.

It is simple in theory, studious in its implementation methodology, and practical in its long-term planning potential.

It is a disciplined process that may not be exciting in its operational minutia, but its focuses on your company's functional DNA needs. There are three steps to the program:

1. Grow revenues by 1% a month from the preceding month

2. Reduce expenses by 1% a month from the preceding month

3. Implement this approach for twelve consecutive months

This model is about the details of running your IT business. To reduce your expenses and increase your sales just 1% each month means that you need to understand the levers and pulleys of each department and how they operate to identify the adjustments needed to maximize business success.

The net gain of this program is a 24% compounded increase in cash flow in one year. If your business model adjustments and changes make sense, carry these suggestions into the succeeding year. This causes a compound effect on your business and positively increases total business revenues and corporate profitability.

By focusing on small identifiable changes and modifications instead of trying to hit home runs, you maximize the underlining management of the levers and pulleys that operate your IT business day to day and increase your success.

It's like batting .400 as a baseball player by hitting single and doubles on a consistent basis instead of aiming for the bleachers.

Where do these department changes come from? Everywhere—improved travel and expense management, increased new business from existing customers, improved marketing expenditure return on investment, setting up company-wide pursuit sales team programs to sell targeted key accounts to increase selling efficiency, enhanced development bench utilization rates, and tighter Profit and Loss analysis of your support and implementation departments.

Small, premeditated changes in your IT business can give you huge changes in your financial success.

The IT business is a pulley-and-lever operation. All departments are interrelated. The sales team can fail because your marketing scares prospects away. Your financials can be off because you priced your IT offering wrong. Your support department and bench utilization costs can be sky high because your sales forecasts are inaccurate.

By managing the intersection of the small details of your high tech business you can accumulatively manage the whole enterprise to increase performance.

> *All you can do is every day, try to solve a*
> *problem and make your company better.*
> *You can't worry about it; you can't panic*
> *when you look at the stock market's decline.*
> *You get frozen like a deer in the headlights.*
> *All you can do is all you can do. If your*
> *cash is about to run out you have to cut your*
> *cash flow. CEOs have to make those*
> *decisions, and live with it, however painful*
> *they might be. You have to act and act now,*
> *and act in the best interests of the company*
> *as a whole, even if that means that some*
> *people in the company who are your friends*
> *have to work somewhere else.*
> *—Larry Ellison*

CEO SUCCESS ACTION STEPS

✓ Determine how to increase revenues 1% per month.

✓ Assess how to cut expenses 1% per month.

✓ Build an annual program based on improved identified income and expense area management to increase corporate cash flow 24%.

Chapter 23

Conclusion

Managing a high tech business as a CEO is not a simple process. It requires patience, communication, personal and professional commitment, metrics analysis, leadership, family commitment, and best-practice guidelines.

Many senior executives struggle with revenue-growth plateaus, employee management, and top-line-revenue enlargement opportunities. Throughout this book, I have outlined specific action steps you can take immediately to manage your business better, grow top-line revenues, and maximize your business efficiencies. These action steps, if taken in totality, offer you a proven process based on best-practice approaches.

Throughout this book, I have given you specific action steps, analysis methods, and strategies you can start implementing today.

To summarize some of the key success drivers I suggested, below are objectives you need to consider in your IT success model:

1. Dominate vertical industries to become horizontal.

2. Sell based on your value, not the competition's price.

3. Manage your company by metrics and P&Ls—not by emotions and hope.

4. Integrate sales, marketing, financial management, operations, and strategy into one revenue program.

5. Put your business value in front of you by forcing your customers to see you as a thought leader (or industry leader) so they take the initiative to buy, instead of you having to sell them.

6. Calculate return on investment for every department and manage your business by it.

7. Maximize your business profitability by increasing your inventory turns and maximizing your clients' lifetime value. If you sell services, your staff and you are the inventory and it must be turned (sold more).

8. Listen to your customers, consultants, employees, competitors, and your gut feeling when making management decisions—but don't let your gut feeling be controlled by your ego.

9. Remember strategy is important, but strategy with execution is better.

10. Never be a generalist. Generalists live in a commodity world. Always be a specialist.

11. Your total corporate revenue should include at least 50% business from new prospects each year. When you are tied only to your existing customers for revenue growth, your success is tied to their ability to buy or not to buy.

12. If you are a family-run business, remember your family members may not be the best employees.

13. The most valuable asset of your business is not the IT products or services you sell—it is the strength of your sales and marketing distribution channels.

14. Strategic partnerships are a key driver for business growth but channel or reseller programs always fail if your direct sales and marketing programs are weak.

15. Mission and vision statements are wasted thought if execution is not implemented.

16. Organic growth is always cheaper than buying companies. Without organic growth processes in place, acquired investments usually fail.

17. Marketing without lead-generation is a wasted investment.

18. Value first, brand second.

19. It is not what you sell—it is what your customers buy.

Procrastination, the bane of us all, may hold you back because the best practices recommended in this book may force you as the CEO to change—but, what is your goal?

Of course, you have a choice. You can build a replicable and scalable business asset, work less, and earn more money—or maintain your status quo.

It is up to you.

Although this is the conclusion of this book it is just the beginning of your company metamorphosis.

I hope you have enjoyed the book. If you have comments on what you read and our methodology and/or the success you have implementing our operating models, please drop me a note.

If you are interested in talking with us one-on-one about any of our high tech business success programs, contact me personally.

To your IT success!

Paul DiModica
CEO/Founder
pdimodica@valueforward.com
www.ValueForward.com
770.632.7647

***Hunt Now or Be Eaten Later*®**

About Paul DiModica

Paul DiModica is the Founder and CEO of the Value Forward Group (www.valueforward.com), a High Tech Business Growth Acceleration firm that integrates marketing, financial management, organizational development design, strategy, operations and sales process into one outbound revenue capture program.

Value Forward works with start-ups, investor funded players, family-run businesses and public companies.

Prior to founding the Value Forward Group in 2001, Paul also founded, e4Speed, a technology managed services, staffing and software project development firm with 45+ employees now owned by a Fortune 1000 company. In 1996, Paul also launched iInform a hospitality automation firm that rented (SaaS) Intelligence (BI) information software to restaurant chains using a touch internet screen browser accessed through the POS system.

Prior to launching his own companies, Paul spent eighteen years working with CEOs in business start-ups, Inc. 500 firms and Fortune 1000 companies. He has held the position of Vice President of Sales and Marketing for Encore Systems, Vice President of Sales for CLS, Senior Vice President of Sales and Marketing at Impressa, Vice President of Operations for Tri-State Systems and Vice President Worldwide of Strategic Development for Renaissance Worldwide (a $900 million public company), reporting directly to the CEO and the Board of Directors. At Renaissance, Paul evaluated the divisional presidents' performances for the board of directors.

Paul has been featured or interviewed by the *New York Times, Investors Daily, Fox News, Selling Power Magazine, Sales and Marketing Magazine, CIO Magazine, CFO Magazine, Entrepreneur Magazine, Training Magazine, Marketing Magazine, Transport Times, Computer World Magazine, Entrepreneur Radio, Chicago Tribune, The Cleveland Sunday Paper, Kansas City Small Business Monthly, The Manager's Intelligence Report, Agent's Sales Journal, Executive Travel Magazine, Wisconsin Professional Journal, Time Compression Technologies Magazine, Minorities and Women Magazine, Broker Agent News, World Fence News, Affluent Magazine, Value Added Partners, The Merchant Magazine, Pennsylvania Business Central Magazine*, and many others.

Sign-up for Our Free Weekly IT Business Success Newsletter

HighTechSuccess
www.hightechsuccess.com

HighTechSuccess is designed for corporate executives in growth directed firms. It provides best practices, case studies and proven methods to increase high tech business success.

High Tech CEO & Team Advisement Services

High Tech 360° Business Success Assessment and Recommendations Program

The Value Forward High Tech 360° Business Model Success and Recommendations Program is a compressive detailed program designed to help companies integrate financial management, marketing, strategy, operations and sales into one outbound revenue capture program. Through our program, we evaluate your business from your prospect's point of view, then from the management team's point of view, and then recommend specific detailed action steps to close the gap between how you see yourself and how prospects see you. Once these recommendations are made, we then work with you and you team in tandem to implement our suggestions.

Value Forward Guided Progress Success (GPS) System

The Value Forward GPS System is a 12-month planned business success program designed to give growth directed clients a step-by-step architectural blueprint to improve their firm's performance.

Using our three sequential stages of analyzing, strategizing and monetizing, we work with senior executives to help build a replicable and scalable revenue capture program based on their goals, their company's core competencies, and industry best practices. A detailed written list of action steps is provided and through a collaborative process, we work with the management team in tandem to execute changes to the business design and operational framework to maximize their corporate success.

IT Team Strategy, Marketing and Sales Training Success Workshops and Advisement Programs

At the Value Forward Group, we offer a broad range of programs and services designed to help sales and marketing teams grow their business revenue and build scalable and replicable revenue capture programs. Our sales training and strategy programs are designed to help you and your team "become a peer in the boardroom, instead of a vendor waiting in the hallway®." Through specific Value Forward tactical techniques and methods, we teach you how to put your business value in front of you so your prospects see you as strategic advisor and take action steps to buy.

Call us today at (770) 632-7647
or visit www.ValueForward.com

We can custom-fit our programs based on your business needs and objectives.

Keynote Speaking, Partner Conferences and Annual Kick-Off Meetings

Have Paul DiModica speak at your next event!

Paul DiModica is a member of the National Speaker's Association (NSA) and speaks worldwide on high tech sales, marketing, strategy and leadership delivering motivational and content-rich presentations that help audiences understand how to increase their personal and corporate performance based on proven strategic and tactical actions they can take immediately. All programs are custom fitted to the client's needs and objectives and combine humor, actionable content and audience engagement.

Paul is available for keynote speaking, kick-off meetings, partner conferences, and company-wide learning. Performance topics include:

- How to Sell Management as a Peer Not a Vendor
- How to Create Value That Buyers Believe

Call us today at 770-632-7647

CPSIA information can be obtained at www.ICGtesting.com
Printed in the USA
LVOW10s0138191113

361711LV00001B/1/P